LEARN CHINESE
VOCABULARY
FOR BEGINNERS

NEW HSK LEVEL 3 VOCABULARY BOOK
MASTER 900+ WORDS IN CONTEXT

Chinese • Pinyin • English

LingLing

www.linglingmandarin.com

My gratitude goes to my wonderful students who study Mandarin with me. You have inspired my writing and provided me with valuable feedback to complete this book. Your support is deeply appreciated!

A special thanks goes to my husband, Phil, who motivated my creation and assisted with editing the book.

Access
FREE AUDIO

SCAN ME

Check the **"ACCESS AUDIO"** chapter for
password and full instructions
(see Table of Contents)

CONTENTS

千　里　之　行
qiān　lǐ　zhī　xíng

始　于　足　下
shǐ　yú　zú　xià

*A journey of a thousand miles
begins with a single step*

- LAOZI -

INTRODUCTION

Congratulations on successfully completing the vocabulary learning in Levels 1 and 2 with my previous books in the **NEW HSK Vocabulary Series!** Your diligent efforts and commitment have brought you this far - a monumental achievement!

Upon completing this book, you will have acquired over 2000 words that complete the Elementary stage, preparing you for the exciting realm of Intermediate Chinese learning. My books in this vocabulary series, covering HSK 4 to 6, await to guide you through learning an additional 3000 words, further enriching your linguistic journey.

WHAT IS THIS BOOK

This comprehensive vocabulary book continues to help you toward confident daily communication. Designed to fortify your language skills, it offers a wide range of essential keywords, specifically covering New HSK Level 3. Even if you are unfamiliar with HSK or are not studying for it directly, rest assured that the key vocabulary and additional words included in the examples are highly relevant to modern Chinese interactions. Expand your linguistic horizons and enhance your ability to engage effectively in real-life conversations with this invaluable resource.

All the keywords are presented in alphabetical order according to the pinyin, each featuring:

- Simplified Chinese characters used in Mainland China
- Pinyin for pronunciation aid
- English definitions
- Complete sentence examples demonstrating usage
- Full English translations
- Downloadable Chinese audio

In many cases where multiple definitions exist for a word, full-sentence examples are provided for each definition.

BONUS CONTENT

Alongside acquiring HSK 3 vocabulary from this book, you'll find a valuable bonus chapter dedicated to honing 20 extra grammar points. These examples employ vocabulary from HSK Level 3, facilitating a swift transition from vocabulary acquisition to crafting fluent, native-sounding sentences.

HOW THIS BOOK WILL HELP

To effectively learn Chinese, simply memorizing words in isolation is insufficient. This book goes beyond vocabulary memorization by providing comprehensive examples that help you master not only the words, but also their correct usage. It introduces common sentence patterns and related language to advance your journey toward Chinese mastery.

Studying the examples and practicing with the provided sentence patterns will establish a strong foundation in everyday Chinese vocabulary. Whether or not you plan to take the HSK exam, this book significantly enhances your conversational abilities. It equips you with the necessary tools to confidently communicate in various contexts, making your learning experience practical and applicable to real-life conversations.

LEVEL UP YOUR LEARNING WITH COMPANION BOOKS

To enhance your Chinese speaking and listening skills, I highly recommend using this book alongside my book, **Chinese Conversations for Beginners**. This combination provides a well-rounded approach to practice and improve your language abilities.

Additionally, if you enjoy engaging stories and want to explore Chinese culture, legends, and folktales, check out my book, **Chinese Stories for Language Learners: Elementary**. It offers an enjoyable way to deepen your language understanding while immersing yourself in Chinese cultural narratives.

FREE DOWNLOADABLE AUDIO

Great news! The Chinese audio files for the book is a FREE gift for you, which you can access from the "Access Audio" page (see table of contents).

NEW HSK LEVEL 3

HSK, short for Hanyu Shuiping Kaoshi (Mandarin Level Examination), is an internationally recognized skill test for non-native Chinese speakers. It is officially introduced by the Chinese government and organized by the Chinese Education Ministry Hanban/Confucius Institutes. The new HSK standard (HSK 3.0) was implemented in July 2021, replacing the old HSK Standard with its 6 levels. The new version features 9 levels, incorporating a more specific classification system, including levels and bands. Compared to its predecessor, the new HSK has been upgraded and expanded, with an increased number of words required for each level.

As a general learner, focusing on levels 1 to 6 will enable you to become an effective Mandarin speaker. Levels 7 and above are specifically designed for advanced learners, such as those intending to pursue Master's or PhD programs in Chinese language studies.

This book presents a concise set of 957 words out of the total 973 words listed for New HSK Level 3. Repetitive words have been eliminated, and some words sharing the same characters (with different pinyin) have been grouped into one word with two categories for display purposes.

LEARN CHINESE WITH A NEW VISION

Chinese, an ancient and vibrant language with a history spanning over 3500 years, offers immense diversity and artistic expression. As one of the world's most spoken languages, mastering Chinese opens doors to countless opportunities in travel, business, and personal growth.

Yet, studying Chinese is more than just learning a language; it's an exploration of a unique mindset and a pathway to new perspectives. By delving into its language and culture, you gain a profound understanding of a rich heritage cultivated over millennia. This lifelong journey fosters personal growth and brings harmony and fulfillment to your life. Embrace the wonders of Chinese, and embark on a transformative voyage of discovery.

HOW TO USE THIS BOOK

Here are some tips to use this book most effectively:

1. **Stick to a fixed routine.** For example, master ten words per day or week - you pick a number and schedule that suits you, but most importantly, stick to it.

2. **Capture the Words.** Write down the key vocabulary in a notebook or type it out digitally, this can enhance your memory of the characters.

3. **Read aloud**, especially the sentence examples. Imagine the context in your head when reading.

4. **Test** yourself by covering the Pinyin and English (using a bookmark for example). If you can read and understand the Chinese on its own, you have memorized it.

5. **Listen** to the audio. Practice imitating the audio and keep listening until you can comprehend the audio without the help of the text.

6. **Review** as often as you can. Repetition is the mother of skill!

7. **Create** your own sentence examples. Practice speaking them aloud, and if possible, use them with a language partner. One becomes a true master through creation!

BELIEVE IN YOURSELF

Never be afraid of making mistakes. In real life, even advanced learners and native speakers make mistakes! Learning from mistakes only makes us grow quicker! So, never let mistakes put you off. Instead, be bold, embrace and learn from them!

SET GOALS AND STAY COMMITTED

Have a committed learning attitude and set goals from small to big will lead you to great achievements in your Chinese learning journey. So stay committed and never give up! Just like this Chinese idiom:

Nothing is impossible to a willing heart

1

VOCABULARY

IN CONTEXT

1 爱心　　　ài xīn　　　**Noun:** compassion

她 很 有 爱 心 ， 常 常 做 慈 善 。
tā hěn yǒu ài xīn　chángcháng zuò cí shàn
She is very compassionate (has a lot of **compassion**) and often does charity work.

2 安排　　　ān pái　　　**Verb:** to arrange
　　　　　　　　　　　　　　　Noun: arrangement

Verb
父 母 安 排 她 跟 小 文 相 亲 。
fù mǔ ān pái tā gēn xiǎo wén xiāng qīn
Her parents **arranged** for her to have a blind date with Xiaowen.

Noun
可 是 ， 她 不 喜 欢 这 个 安 排 。
kě shì tā bù xǐ huān zhè gè ān pái
However, she doesn't like this **arrangement**.

3 安装　　　ān zhuāng　　　**Verb:** to install

我 打 算 在 客 厅 里 安 装 空 调 。
wǒ dǎ suàn zài kè tīng lǐ ān zhuāng kōng tiáo
I am going **to install** an air conditioner in the living room.

4 按　　　àn　　　**Verb:** to press

我 刚 刚 听 到 有 人 按 门 铃 了 。
wǒ gānggāng tīng dào yǒu rén àn mén líng le
I just heard someone ring (**press**) the doorbell.

5 按(照)　　　àn zhào　　　**Preposition:** according to

请 按 照 顾 客 的 需 要 发 订 单 。
qǐng àn zhào gù kè de xū yào fā dìng dān
Please send orders **according to** the customer's requirements.

6a 把   bǎ

Preposition: describe an action (把 + noun + verb)

qǐng bǎ diàn shì guān le
请 **把** 电 视 关 了 。
Please turn off the TV.

6b 把   bǎ

Classifier for things with handles

zhuō shàng yǒu yì bǎ dāo hé yì bǎ shàn zi
桌 上 有 一 **把** 刀 和 一 **把** 扇 子 。
There is **a** knife and **a** fan on the table.

7 把握   bǎ wò

Verb: to seize; to hold
Noun: assurance

Verb
wǒ yào bǎ wò zhè cì miàn shì de jī huì
我 要 **把 握** 这 次 面 试 的 机 会 。
I want **to seize** the opportunity of this interview.

Noun
nǐ yǒu bǎ wò chéng gōng ma
你 有 **把 握** 成 功 吗 ？
Do you have **assurance** to succeed?

8 白   bái

Adverb: in vain; waste effort
Adjective: white

Adv.
wǒ bái děng le tā yí gè xiǎo shí
我 **白** 等 了 他 一 个 小 时 。
I waited for him for an hour **in vain**.

Adj.
tā yǐ jīng kāi shǐ yǒu bái tóu fa le
他 已 经 开 始 有 **白** 头 发 了 。
He has started to have **white** hair.

9 白菜   bái cài

Noun: Chinese cabbage (white cabbage)

wǒ hěn ài chī zhū ròu bái cài bāo zi
我 很 爱 吃 猪 肉 **白 菜** 包 子 。
I love to eat pork and **cabbage** buns.

10 班(级)   bān jí   **Noun:** class

wǒ zuì hǎo de péng yǒu hé wǒ zài tóng yí gè bān jí
我 最 好 的 朋 友 和 我 在 同 一 个 **班 级** 。
My best friend is in the same **class** as me.

11 搬   bān   **Verb:** to move

qǐng bǎ zhuō zi bān dào kè tīng
请 把 桌 子 **搬** 到 客 厅 。
Please **move** the table to the living room.

12 搬家   bān jiā   **Verb:** to move house

wǒ men xià gè yuè huì bān jiā dào lún dūn
我 们 下 个 月 会 **搬 家** 到 伦 敦 。
We will **move house** to London next month.

13 板   bǎn   **Noun:** board; shutter; plank

wǒ xiǎng zài xīn jiā ān zhuāng mù bǎn
我 想 在 新 家 安 装 木 **板** 。
I want to install wooden **planks** in my new home.

14 办(理)   bàn lǐ   **Verb:** to apply; to handle

tā qù dà shǐ guǎn bàn lǐ qiān zhèng le
他 去 大 使 馆 **办 理** 签 证 了 。
He went to the embassy **to apply** for a visa.

15 保   bǎo   **Verb:** to maintain

zhè gè fàn hé kě yǐ bǎo wēn
这 个 饭 盒 可 以 **保 温** 。
This lunch box can **maintain** the temperature.

16 保安   bǎo ān   **Noun:** security guard

tā men shì bǎo ān bú shì jǐng chá
他 们 是 **保 安**，不 是 警 察 。
They are **security guards**, not police.

17 保持   bǎo chí   **Verb:** to keep

tā men fēn shǒu hòu réng rán bǎo chí lián xì
他 们 分 手 后 仍 然 **保 持** 联 系 。
They still **kept** in touch after breaking up.

18 保存   bǎo cún   **Verb:** to preserve; to hold

wǒ yòng bīng xiāng bǎo cún fàn cài hé yǐn liào
我 用 冰 箱 **保 存** 饭 菜 和 饮 料 。
I use the refrigerator **to preserve** meals and drinks.

19 保护   bǎo hù   **Verb:** to protect   **Noun:** protection

Verb
tā huì gōng fu yí dìng kě yǐ bǎo hù nǐ
他 会 功 夫 ， 一 定 可 以 **保 护** 你 。
He can do kung fu and can definitely **protect** you.

Noun
kě shì wǒ bù xū yào tā de bǎo hù
可 是 ， 我 不 需 要 他 的 **保 护** 。
However, I don't need his **protection**.

20 保留   bǎo liú   **Verb:** to keep (retain)

fù qīn qù shì hòu mǔ qīn bǎo liú le tā de
父 亲 去 世 后 ， 母 亲 **保 留** 了 他 的
yī fú
衣 服 。
After my father died, my mother **kept** his clothes.

21 保险 bǎo xiǎn **Noun:** insurance

wǒ yào wèi wǒ nǚ ér hé ér zi mǎi rén shēn bǎo xiǎn
我 要 为 我 女 儿 和 儿 子 买 人 身 保 险 。
I want to buy life **insurance** for my daughter and son.

22 保证 bǎo zhèng **Verb:** to guarantee; to promise

wǒ nán péng yǒu bǎo zhèng le huì jiè dú
我 男 朋 友 保 证 了 会 戒 毒 。
My boyfriend has **promised** to quit drugs.

23 报名 bào míng **Verb:** to sign up

wǒ bào míng le yí gè wǎng qiú kè chéng
我 报 名 了 一 个 网 球 课 程 。
I **signed up** for a tennis lesson.

24 报到 bào dào **Verb:** to register (check in)

xīn yuán gōng děi qù rén shì bù mén bào dào
新 员 工 得 去 人 事 部 门 报 到 。
New employees need to go the HR department to **register**.

25 报道 bào dào **Verb:** to report (news) **Noun:** report

Verb
jì zhě qù xiàn chǎng bào dào le shì gù
记 者 去 现 场 报 道 了 事 故 。
Journalists went to the scene **to report** the accident.

Noun
zhè gè bào dào shàng le tóu tiáo
这 个 报 道 上 了 头 条 。
This **report** hit the headlines.

26 报告   bào gào   **Noun:** presentation; report

lǎo bǎn duì wǒ de gōng zuò bào gào hěn mǎn yì
老 板 对 我 的 工 作 **报 告** 很 满 意 。
The boss is very satisfied with my work **report**.

27 北部   běi bù   **Noun:** north

tā men cóng nán bù bān jiā dào le běi bù
他 们 从 南 部 搬 家 到 了 **北 部** 。
They moved house from the south to the **north**.

28 背   bēi   **Verb:** to carry

wǒ xiǎo de shí hòu wǒ bà cháng cháng bēi wǒ qù
我 小 的 时 候 ， 我 爸 常 常 **背** 我 去
yòu ér yuán
幼 儿 园 。
When I was young, my dad used **to carry** me to kindergarten.

29 背   bèi   **Noun:** back of the body; backside of an object

wǒ bèi tòng yī shēng jiàn yì wǒ zuò yú jiā
我 **背** 痛 ， 医 生 建 议 我 做 瑜 伽 。
My **back** hurts, the doctor suggested that I do yoga.

30 背后   bèi hòu   **Noun:** behind; at the back

yī yuàn de bèi hòu yǒu yí gè gōng yuán hé yì tiáo hé
医 院 的 **背 后** 有 一 个 公 园 和 一 条 河 。
There is a park and a river **behind** the hospital.

31 被   bèi   **Preposition:** indicate passive action (被 + verb)

wǒ nǚ péng yǒu de shǒu jī bèi tōu le
我 女 朋 友 的 手 机 **被** 偷 了 。
My girlfriend's cell phone **was** stolen.

32 被子   bèi zi   **Noun:** quilt; cover

wǒ yòng xǐ yī jī xǐ bèi zi hé yī fu
我 用 洗 衣 机 洗 **被 子** 和 衣 服 。
I use a washing machine to wash **quilts** and clothes.

33 本来   běn lái   **Adverb:** originally (planned to do but didn't do it)

tā men běn lái dǎ suàn jié hūn dàn shì fàng qì le
他 们 **本 来** 打 算 结 婚 ， 但 是 放 弃 了 。
They **originally** planned to get married, but gave it up.

34 本领   běn lǐng   **Noun:** ability

nǐ de běn lǐng yuè qiáng jiù yuè yǒu jī huì shēng zhí
你 的 **本 领** 越 强 ， 就 越 有 机 会 升 职 。
The stronger your **ability**, the more opportunities you have to be promoted.

35 本事   běn shi   **Noun:** skill

chéng gōng de rén dōu shì yǒu běn shi de rén
成 功 的 人 都 是 有 **本 事** 的 人 。
Successful people are all people with **skills**.

36 比较 bǐ jiào

Verb: to compare
Adverb: relatively

Verb
gēn bié rén bǐ jiào cái fù hěn méi yì si
跟 别 人 比 较 财 富 很 没 意 思 。
Comparing wealth with others is pointless.

Adv.
wǒ qián nǚ yǒu de xìng gé bǐ jiào nèi xiàng
我 前 女 友 的 性 格 比 较 内 向 。
My ex-girlfriend's personality was **relatively** introverted.

37 比例 bǐ lì

Noun: proportion

tā de shēn gāo hé tǐ zhòng méi yǒu bǐ lì
她 的 身 高 和 体 重 没 有 比 例 。
Her height and weight are out of **proportion**.

38 比赛 bǐ sài

Noun: match; competition

wǒ bù xiǎng cuò guò shì jiè bēi zú qiú bǐ sài
我 不 想 错 过 世 界 杯 足 球 比 赛 。
I don't want to miss the World Cup football **matches**.

39 必然 bì rán

Adjective: inevitable

wǒ jué de tā men de lí hūn shì bì rán de
我 觉 得 他 们 的 离 婚 是 必 然 的 。
I think their divorce is **inevitable**.

40 必要 bì yào

Adjective: necessary

wǒ zài wèi miàn shì zuò bì yào de zhǔn bèi
我 在 为 面 试 做 必 要 的 准 备 。
I'm making the **necessary** preparations for the interview.

41 变化　biàn huà　**Noun:** change

yǒu shí hòu, shì chǎng jīng jì de biàn huà hěn dà
有 时 候 ，市 场 经 济 的 **变 化** 很 大 。
Sometimes, the **changes** in the market economy are big.

42 变为　biàn wéi　**Verb:** to change into

wǒ men yào bǎ yā lì biàn wéi dòng lì
我 们 要 把 压 力 **变 为** 动 力 。
We need to **turn** pressure **into** motivation.

43 标题　biāo tí　**Noun:** title; heading

nǐ xiě guò zhè yàng de zuò wén biāo tí ma
你 写 过 这 样 的 作 文 **标 题** 吗 ？
Have you ever written a composition **title** like this?

44 标准　biāo zhǔn　**Noun:** standard; criteria　**Adjective:** up to standard

nǐ de zé ǒu biāo zhǔn shì shén me
Noun　你 的 择 偶 **标 准** 是 什 么 ？
What is your spouse selection **criteria**?

tā de fā yīn bú tài biāo zhǔn
Adj.　他 的 发 音 不 太 **标 准** 。
His pronunciation is not **up to the standard**.

45 表达　biǎo dá　**Verb:** to express　**Noun:** expression

tā yòng zhè shǒu gē biāo dá le duì tā de ài
Verb　他 用 这 首 歌 **表 达** 了 对 她 的 爱 。
He used this song **to express** his love for her.

zhè zhǒng biǎo dá hěn làng màn
Noun　这 种 **表 达** 很 浪 漫 。
This type of **expression** is very romantic.

46 表格　　biǎo gé　　**Noun:** form

^{má} ^{fán} ^{nǐ} ^{tián} ^{yí} ^{xià} ^{zhè} ^{zhāng} ^{biǎo} ^{gé}
麻 烦 你 填 一 下 这 张 表 格 。
May I trouble you to fill out this **form**.

47 表面　　biǎo miàn　　**Noun:** surface

^{tā} ^{biǎo} ^{miàn} ^{shàng} ^{ài} ^{lǎo} ^{pó} ^{dàn} ^{shì} ^{cháng} ^{cháng} ^{chū} ^{guǐ}
他 表 面 上 爱 老 婆 ， 但 是 常 常 出 轨 。
He loves his wife on the **surface**, but often cheats on her.

48 表明　　biǎo míng　　**Verb:** to indicate

^{zhè} ^{biǎo} ^{míng} ^{tā} ^{bú} ^{shì} ^{gè} ^{hǎo} ^{lǎo} ^{gōng}
这 表 明 他 不 是 个 好 老 公 。
This **indicates** that he is not a good husband.

49 表现　　biǎo xiàn　　**Verb:** to perform
Noun: performance; display

Verb
^{tā} ^{zài} ^{gōng} ^{zuò} ^{shàng} ^{biǎo} ^{xiàn} ^{de} ^{yuè} ^{lái} ^{yuè} ^{hǎo}
他 在 工 作 上 表 现 得 越 来 越 好 ！
He **performs** better and better at work!

Noun
^{jīng} ^{lǐ} ^{duì} ^{tā} ^{de} ^{biǎo} ^{xiàn} ^{hěn} ^{mǎn} ^{yì}
经 理 对 他 的 表 现 很 满 意 ！
The manager is very pleased with his **performance**!

50 表演　　biǎo yǎn　　**Verb:** to perform (a show)
Noun: performance

Verb
^{wǒ} ^{péng} ^{yǒu} ^{míng} ^{wǎn} ^{huì} ^{zài} ^{jù} ^{yuàn} ^{biǎo} ^{yǎn}
我 朋 友 明 晚 会 在 剧 院 表 演 。
My friend will **perform** in the theater tomorrow night.

Noun
^{wǒ} ^{hěn} ^{qī} ^{dài} ^{tā} ^{de} ^{biǎo} ^{yǎn}
我 很 期 待 他 的 表 演 。
I'm looking forward to his **performance**.

51 并   bìng   **Conjunction:** and; besides
Adverb: actually

Con.
wǒ ài guò tā bìng xiǎng hé tā zài yì qǐ
我 爱 过 他 **并** 想 和 他 在 一 起 。
I loved him, **and** wanted to be with him.

Adv.
kě shì wǒ bìng bù zhī dào tā yǐ jīng jié hūn le
可 是 ， 我 **并** 不 知 道 他 已 经 结 婚 了 。
However, I **actually** didn't know he was married.

52 并且   bìng qiě   **Conjunction:** and; furthermore

kàn lái tā bù chéng shí bìng qiě bù kě kào
看 来 他 不 诚 实 ， **并 且** 不 可 靠 。
It looks like he is dishonest **and** unreliable.

53 播出   bō chū   **Verb:** to broadcast; to air

zhè bù diàn shì jù bō chū hòu hěn huǒ
这 部 电 视 剧 **播 出** 后 很 火 ！
After the TV series **aired**, it became very popular!

54 播放   bō fàng   **Verb:** to play (videos/music)

nǐ yòng shén me shǒu jī chéng xù bō fàng yīn yuè
你 用 什 么 手 机 程 序 **播 放** 音 乐 ？
Which mobile app do you use **to play** music?

55 不必   bú bì   **Adverb:** need not; not have to

bú bì dān xīn wǒ zhī dào zěn me chǔ lǐ
不 必 担 心 ！ 我 知 道 怎 么 处 理 。
No need to worry! I know how to deal with it.

56 不断   bú duàn   **Adverb:** constantly

wèi le zhào gù wǒ men   tā bú duàn nǔ lì zhèng qián
为 了 照 顾 我 们 ， 他 **不 断** 努 力 挣 钱 。
In order to take care of us, he is **constantly** working hard to earn money.

57 不论   bú lùn   **Conjunction:** whether … or; no matter

bú lùn tā yǒu méi yǒu qián   wǒ dōu bù lí kāi tā
不 论 他 有 没 有 钱 ， 我 都 不 离 开 他 。
No matter he has money or not, I will not leave him.

58 补   bǔ   **Verb:** to repair; to mend

wǒ zài bāng tā bǔ kù zi hé wà zi
我 在 帮 他 **补** 裤 子 和 袜 子 。
I am helping him **mend** his trousers and socks.

59 补充   bǔ chōng   **Verb:** to add; to supplement

wǒ yào bǔ chōng yí xià tǎo lùn jié guǒ
我 要 **补 充** 一 下 讨 论 结 果 。
I would like **to supplement** the results of the discussion.

60 不安   bù ān   **Adjective:** uneasy; unpeaceful

tā yì tiān dōu bù jiē diàn huà   wǒ hěn bù ān
他 一 天 都 不 接 电 话 ， 我 很 **不 安** 。
He didn't answer the phone all day and I feel very **uneasy**.

61 不得不   bù dé bù   **Adverb:** cannot but; have to

rú guǒ tā shī zōng   wǒ jiù bù dé bù bào jǐng
如 果 他 失 踪 ， 我 就 **不 得 不** 报 警 。
If he goes missing, I'll **have to** call the police.

62 不光　bù guāng　**Conjunction:** not only; not just

bù guāng shì nǐ ，　wǒ yě hěn dān xīn 。
不光是你，我也很担心。
Not only you, I am also worried.

63 不仅　bù jǐn　**Conjunction:** not only

tā bù jǐn huì kāi chē ，　ér qiě huì kāi fēi jī 。
他**不仅**会开车，**而且**会开飞机。
He can **not only** drive a car, **but also** fly a plane.

64 布　bù　**Noun:** cloth

wǒ xiǎng mǎi zhè kuài bù zuò chuāng lián 。
我想买这块**布**做窗帘。
I want to buy this **cloth** to make curtains.

65 步　bù　**Noun:** step; foot

nǐ jué de wǒ xià yí bù yīng gāi zěn me zuò ？
你觉得我下一**步**应该怎么做？
What do you think I should do for the next **step**?

66 部　bù　**Noun:** unit; part

wǒ de jiā xiāng zài zhōng guó nán bù 。
我的家乡在中国南**部**。
My hometown is in the southern **part** of China.

67 部(门)　bù mén　**Noun:** department

rén shì bù mén zài zuǒ biān ，　xiāo shòu bù mén zài yòu biān 。
人事**部门**在左边，销售**部门**在右边。
The HR **department** is on the left and the sales **department** is on the right.

68 部长　bù zhǎng　**Noun:** minister

wǒ jiè shào yí xià, zhè shì wài jiāo bù zhǎng chén xiān shēng
我 介 绍 一 下 ， 这 是 外 交 **部 长** 陈 先 生。
Let me introduce, this is the **Minister** of Foreign Affairs, Mr Chen.

69 才能　cái néng　**Noun:** talent; ability

wǒ pìn yòng tā, shì yīn wèi xīn shǎng tā de cái néng
我 聘 用 他 ， 是 因 为 欣 赏 他 的 **才 能**。
I hired him because I admired his **talent**.

70 采取　cǎi qǔ　**Verb:** to take (advice)

zǒng cái méi yǒu cǎi qǔ cái wù zǒng jiān de jiàn yì
总 裁 没 有 **采 取** 财 务 总 监 的 建 议。
The CEO did not **take** the advice of the CFO.

71 采用　cǎi yòng　**Verb:** to put to use; to implement

tā bù dǎ suàn zài gōng sī cǎi yòng zhè gè jì shù
他 不 打 算 在 公 司 **采 用** 这 个 技 术。
He does not intend **to implement** this technology in the company.

72 彩色　cǎi sè　**Noun:** multicolor; colorful

wǒ mǎi le hěn duō cǎi sè de qì qiú
我 买 了 很 多 **彩 色** 的 气 球。
I bought a lot of **colorful** balloons.

73 曾经　céng jīng　**Adverb:** once; in the past

wǒ céng jīng zhēn xīn ài guò tā
我 **曾 经** 真 心 爱 过 她。
I **once** truly loved her.

74 产生　　chǎn shēng　　**Verb:** to bring about

wǒ méi yǒu duì tā chǎn shēng guò huái yí
我 没 有 对 她 **产 生** 过 怀 疑 。
I have never had any doubts (**brought**) about her.

75 长城　　cháng chéng　　**Noun:** The Great Wall

xià gè yuè wǒ hé tóng bàn men huì qù pá cháng chéng
下 个 月 我 和 同 伴 们 会 去 爬 **长 城** 。
Next month, my companions and I will climb **The Great Wall**.

76 长处　　cháng chù　　**Noun:** strength; strong point

měi gè rén dōu yǒu cháng chù hé duǎn chù
每 个 人 都 有 **长 处** 和 短 处 。
Everyone has **strengths** and weaknesses.

77 长期　　cháng qī　　**Noun:** long-term; over a long period of time

wǒ dǎ suàn cháng qī xué zhōng wén
我 打 算 **长 期** 学 中 文 。
I plan to study Chinese **long-term**.

78 厂　　chǎng　　**Noun:** factory; mill

tā shì zhè gè chǎng de chǎng zhǎng
她 是 这 个 **厂** 的 **厂** 长 。
She is the boss (**factory** senior) of this **factory**.

79 场合　　chǎng hé　　**Noun:** occasion

tā zài shāng wù chǎng hé chuān de hěn zhèng shì
她 在 商 务 **场 合** 穿 得 很 正 式 。
She dresses formally for business **occasions**.

80 场所   chǎng suǒ   **Noun: place**

bié zài gōng gòng chǎng suǒ mà rén
别 在 公 共 **场 所** 骂 人 ！
Don't scold at people in public **places**!

81 超(级)   chāo jí   **Adverb: super; extremely**

nà gè chāo mó chāo jí xìng gǎn
那 个 **超** 模 **超 级** 性 感 ！
That **super**model is **super** sexy!

82 朝   cháo   **Preposition: towards**
Noun: dynasty

Pre.
cháo qián zǒu rán hòu yòu zhuǎn jiù dào le
朝 前 走 ， 然 后 右 转 ， 就 到 了 。
Go ahead (**towards** front), then turn right and you're there.

Noun
táng cháo shì zhōng guó lì shǐ shàng zuì chū míng de
唐 **朝** 是 中 国 历 史 上 最 出 名 的 。
The Tang **Dynasty** is the most famous in Chinese history.

83 吵   chǎo   **Verb: to make a noise**
Adjective: noisy

Verb
bié chǎo hái zi zài shuì jiào
别 **吵** ， 孩 子 在 睡 觉 。
Don't **make noise**, the child is sleeping.

Adj.
zhè tiáo jiē rén tài duō fēi cháng chǎo
这 条 街 人 太 多 ， 非 常 **吵** ！
There are too many people on this street and it is very **noisy**!

84 吵(架)   chǎo jià   **Verb: to quarrel**

wǒ zuó tiān gēn nán péng yǒu chǎo jià le
我 昨 天 跟 男 朋 友 **吵 架** 了 。
I **quarreled** with my boyfriend yesterday.

85 衬衫　　chèn shān　　**Noun:** shirt

tā de bái chèn shān shàng yǒu kǒu hóng yìn
他 的 白 衬 衫 上 有 口 红 印 。

There are lipstick marks on his white **shirt**.

86 衬衣　　chèn yī　　**Noun:** undergarment

wǒ zài máo yī xià miàn chuān le chèn yī
我 在 毛 衣 下 面 穿 了 衬 衣 。

I am wearing an **undergarment** under the sweater.

87 称为　　chēng wéi　　**Verb:** to be called; to be known as

lǐ xiǎo lóng bèi chēng wéi wǔ shù dà shī
李 小 龙 被 称 为 武 术 大 师 。

Bruce Lee was **known as** a master of martial arts.

88 成功　　chéng gōng　　**Verb:** to succeed　**Noun:** success

Verb
nǔ lì duō nián hòu tā zhōng yú chéng gōng le
努 力 多 年 后 ， 他 终 于 成 功 了 。

After years of hard work, he finally **succeeded**.

Noun
wǒ wèi tā de chéng gōng jiāo ào
我 为 他 的 成 功 骄 傲 ！

I am proud of his **success**!

89 成果　　chéng guǒ　　**Noun:** great result

zhè shì tuán duì hé zuò de chéng guǒ
这 是 团 队 合 作 的 成 果 。

This is the **great result** of teamwork.

90 成就   chéng jiù   **Noun:** achievement

chéng jiù lái zì nǔ lì   zhì huì hé nài xīn
成就来自努力、智慧和耐心。
Achievement comes from hard work, wisdom and patience.

91 成立   chéng lì   **Verb:** to establish

wǒ de mèng xiǎng shì chéng lì zì jǐ de gōng sī
我的梦想是成立自己的公司。
My dream is **to establish** my own company.

92 成熟   chéng shú   **Adjective:** mature

wǒ hěn gāo xìng yīn wèi tā yuè lái yuè chéng shú
我很高兴，因为他越来越成熟。
I'm happy because he's getting more and more **mature**.

93 成员   chéng yuán   **Noun:** member

lǐ xiān shēng shì dǒng shì huì de chéng yuán
李先生是董事会的成员。
Mr. Li is a **member** of the board of directors.

94 (成)长   chéng zhǎng   **Verb:** to grow

wǒ de yīng huā shù chéng zhǎng de hěn kuài
我的樱花树成长得很快。
My cherry blossom tree is **growing** very fast.

95 城   chéng   **Noun:** city; town

wǒ tīng shuō sì chuān shěng yǒu sān shí wǔ gè chéng
我听说四川省有三十五个城。
I heard that there are thirty-five **cities** in Sichuan Province.

96 城市　　chéng shì　　**Noun:** city

zhè shì zuì dà de lǚ yóu chéng shì
这 是 最 大 的 旅 游 **城 市** 。
This is the largest tourist **city**.

97 程度　　chéng dù　　**Noun:** degree; level

wǒ fù mǔ de jiào yù chéng dù bù gāo
我 父 母 的 教 育 **程 度** 不 高 。
My parents' education **level** is not high.

98 持续　　chí xù　　**Verb:** to continue; to sustain

zhèng fǔ xī wàng jīng jì chí xù fā zhǎn
政 府 希 望 经 济 **持 续** 发 展 。
The government hopes the economy **continues** to develop.

99 充满　　chōng mǎn　　**Verb:** to fill; to be full of

nǐ ràng wǒ de xīn chōng mǎn xìng fú
你 让 我 的 心 **充 满** 幸 福 。
You make my heart **full of** happiness.

100a 重　　chóng　　**Verb:** to repeat; to overlap

nǐ xiě cuò le qǐng chóng xiě
你 写 错 了 ， 请 **重** 写 。
You wrote incorrectly, please rewrite (**repeat** writing).

100b 重　　zhòng　　**Adjective:** heavy

wǒ de xíng lǐ xiāng hěn zhòng bāo hěn qīng
我 的 行 李 箱 很 **重** ， 包 很 轻 。
My suitcase is **heavy** and my bag is light.

101 初   chū   **Noun:** beginning; start

wǒ de kǎo shì zài nián chū hé nián dǐ
我 的 考 试 在 年 **初** 和 年 底 。
My exams are at the **beginning** of the year and end of the year.

102 初一   chū yī   **Noun:** first grade of middle school; first day of lunar year

wǒ mèi mei shàng chū yī   wǒ dì di shàng chū èr
我 妹 妹 上 **初 一** , 我 弟 弟 上 初 二 。
My younger sister is in the **first grade**, my younger brother is in the second grade.

zài nián chū yī   zhōng guó rén huì zài jiā lǐ péi
在 (年) **初 一** , 中 国 人 会 在 家 里 陪
jiā rén
家 人 。
On the **first day of lunar new year**, Chinese people will stay at home with their families.

103 初步   chū bù   **Adjective:** preliminary

tǎo lùn de chū bù jié guǒ shì shén me
讨 论 的 **初 步** 结 果 是 什 么 ？
What were the **preliminary** results of the discussions?

104 初级   chū jí   **Adjective:** elementary

wǒ mǎi le yì běn chū jí zhōng wén gù shi shū
我 买 了 一 本 **初 级** 中 文 故 事 书 。
I bought an **elementary** Chinese story book.

105 初中   chū zhōng   **Noun:** middle school

wǒ zài niǔ yuē shàng le chū zhōng hé gāo zhōng
我 在 纽 约 上 了 **初 中** 和 高 中 。
I went to **middle school** and high school in New York.

106 除了　chú le　Preposition: except

chú le tā, wǒ men dōu bù zhī dào jīng lǐ de gōng zī
除了他，我们都不知道经理的工资。
Except for him, none of us know the manager's salary.

107 处理　chǔ lǐ　Verb: to handle

lǐng dǎo cháng cháng xū yào chǔ lǐ yuán gōng wèn tí
领导常常需要处理员工问题。
Leaders often need **to deal** with employee issues.

108 传　chuán　Verb: to pass on; to transmit

fù wēng yào bǎ cái chǎn chuán gěi sān gè zǐ nǚ
富翁要把财产传给三个子女。
The rich man wants **to pass on** his wealth to his three children.

109 传播　chuán bō　Verb: to spread

dài kǒu zhào shì wèi le jiǎn shǎo bìng dú chuán bō
戴口罩是为了减少病毒传播。
Wearing masks is to reduce the virus **spreading**.

110 传来　chuán lái　Verb: to come from

zhè tiáo xiāo xī shì cóng nǎ lǐ chuán lái de
这条消息是从哪里传来的？
Where did this message **come from**?

111 传说　chuán shuō　Noun: legend; tale

wǒ xǐ huān dú mín jiān chuán shuō, nǐ ne
我喜欢读民间传说，你呢？
I love reading folk**tales**, how about you?

112 创新   chuàng xīn   **Verb:** to innovate
Noun: innovation

Verb

wǒ men yào bú duàn chuàng xīn   tí gāo zhì liàng
我 们 要 不 断 **创 新** ， 提 高 质 量 。
We must continue to **innovate** and improve quality.

Noun

gōng sī de lǐng dǎo men hěn kàn zhòng chuàng xīn
公 司 的 领 导 们 很 看 重 **创 新**。
Company leaders place a high value on **innovation**.

113 创业   chuàng yè   **Verb:** to start a business

chuàng yè hěn nán   chuàng yè zhě yě hěn shǎo
创 业 很 难 ， **创 业 者** 也 很 少 。
Starting a business is hard, there are very few **entrepreneurs**.

114 创造   chuàng zào   **Verb:** to create

chuàng zào qí jī de rén dōu shì tiān cái
创 造 奇 迹 的 人 都 是 天 才 。
People who **create** miracles are geniuses.

115 创作   chuàng zuò   **Verb:** to create (literary work)
Noun: creation (literature)

Verb

dà xué gǔ lì xué shēng men duō chuàng zuò
大 学 鼓 励 学 生 们 多 **创 作** 。
Universities encourage students **to create** more.

Noun

wǒ hěn xǐ huān tā de chuàng zuò fēng gé
我 很 喜 欢 她 的 **创 作** 风 格 。
I like the style of her **creation**.

116 从来   cóng lái   **Adverb:** always (from beginning)

tīng shuō   tā cóng lái dōu shì dān shēn
听 说 ， 他 **从 来** 都 是 单 身 。
I heard that he has **always** been single.

117 从前　　cóng qián　　**Noun:** long ago

zhè gè yì wàn fù wēng cóng qián shì gè yú fū
这 个 亿 万 富 翁 **从 前** 是 个 渔 夫 。
This billionaire was a fisherman **long ago**.

118 从事　　cóng shì　　**Verb:** to be engaged in (jobs)

dāng shí， tā zhǐ cóng shì mài yú
当 时 ， 他 只 **从 事** 卖 鱼 。
At that time, he was only **engaged in** selling fish.

119 村(子)　　cūn zi　　**Noun:** village

tā de cūn zi jiào xiǎo yú cūn
他 的 **村 子** 叫 小 渔 **村** 。
His **village** is called Small Fishing **Village**.

120 存　　cún　　**Verb:** to deposit; to save

wǒ měi gè yuè zài yín háng kǎ shàng cún wǔ bǎi měi yuán
我 每 个 月 在 银 行 卡 上 **存** 五 百 美 元 。
I **save** five hundred dollars a month in my bank card.

121 存在　　cún zài　　**Verb:** to exist　**Noun:** existence

Verb
tā men de hūn yīn cún zài dà wèn tí
他 们 的 婚 姻 **存 在** 大 问 题 。
There are big problems **existing** in their marriage.

Noun
bú yào hū shì wèn tí de cún zài
不 要 忽 视 问 题 的 **存 在** 。
Don't ignore the **existence** of problems.

122 错误　　　cuò wù　　　**Noun:** mistake; error

tā　pà　diū　liǎn　　bù　gǎn　chéng　rèn　cuò　wù
他　怕　丢　脸，　不　敢　承　认　错　误。
He was afraid of losing face and dared not admit his **mistakes**.

123 达到　　　dá dào　　　**Verb:** to achieve; to reach

wǒ　de　zhōng　wén　kuài　dá　dào　zhōng　jí　shuǐ　píng　le
我　的　中　文　快　达　到　中　级　水　平　了。
My Chinese will **reach** intermediate level soon.

124 打破　　　dǎ pò　　　**Verb:** to break; to smash

wǒ　de　gǒu　bù　xiǎo　xīn　dǎ　pò　le　wǎn
我　的　狗　不　小　心　打　破　了　碗。
My dog accidentally **broke** the bowl.

125 打听　　　dǎ ting　　　**Verb:** to inquire about

nǐ　kě　yǐ　xiàng　dāng　dì　rén　dǎ　ting　zhè　jiàn　shì
你　可　以　向　当　地　人　打　听　这　件　事。
You can **inquire about** this matter from the locals.

126 大概　　　dà gài　　　**Adjective:** general
　　　　　　　　　　　　　　　Adverb: generally

Adj.
tā　men　duì　zhè　jiàn　shì　yǒu　dà　gài　de　liǎo　jiě
他　们　对　这　件　事　有　大　概　的　了　解。
They have a **general** idea of the matter.

Adv.
wǒ　dà　gài　tīng　dǒng　le
我　大　概　听　懂　了。
I **generally** understand.

127 大使馆   dà shǐ guǎn   **Noun:** embassy

nǐ qù guò lún dūn de zhōng guó dà shǐ guǎn ma
你 去 过 伦 敦 的 中 国 **大 使 馆** 吗？
Have you been to the Chinese **embassy** in London?

128 大约   dà yuē   **Adverb:** about; approximately

táng rén jiē dà yuē yǒu sān shí jiā zhōng cān guǎn
唐 人 街 **大 约** 有 三 十 家 中 餐 馆。
There are **about** thirty Chinese restaurants in Chinatown.

129 大夫   dài fu   **Noun:** doctor

tā shì yí wèi zhù míng de zhōng yī dài fu
他 是 一 位 著 名 的 中 医 **大 夫**。
He is a famous **doctor** of Chinese medicine.

130 代   dài   **Preposition:** for; on behalf of

qǐng nǐ dài wǒ xiàng nǐ fù mǔ wèn hòu
请 你 **代** 我 向 你 父 母 问 候。
Please send my greetings to your parents **for** me.

131 代表   dài biǎo   **Verb:** to represent
Noun: representative

Verb
zhōng qiū jié de yuán yuè dài biǎo tuán yuán
中 秋 节 的 圆 月 **代 表** 团 圆。
The full moon on Mid-Autumn Festival **represents** reunion.

Noun
qǐng gōng sī de dài biǎo zài zhè lǐ qiān zì
请 公 司 的 **代 表** 在 这 里 签 字。
May I ask the **representative** of the company to sign here.

132 代表团　　　dài biǎo tuán　　**Noun:** delegation; mission

měi guó dài biǎo tuán yǐ jīng dào dá jī chǎng le
美 国 代 表 团 已 经 到 达 机 场 了 。
The American **delegation** has arrived at the airport.

133 带动　　　dài dòng　　**Verb:** to spur; to drive

dài dòng dà jiā hé zuò de shì shuāng yíng
带 动 大 家 合 作 的 是 双 赢 。
Driving everyone to cooperate is a win-win situation.

134 带领　　　dài lǐng　　**Verb:** to lead

zǒng jīng lǐ dài lǐng bù mén lǐng dǎo men kāi huì
总 经 理 带 领 部 门 领 导 们 开 会 。
The CEO **leads** the department leaders to a meeting.

135 单元　　　dān yuán　　**Noun:** unit

wǒ de gōng yù zài èr dān yuán wǔ lóu shí hào
我 的 公 寓 在 二 单 元 五 楼 十 号 。
My apartment is at No. 10, 5th Floor, **Unit** 2.

136 当初　　　dāng chū　　**Noun:** at that time; back then

dāng chū wǒ de nǚ péng yǒu jiù zhù zài gé bì
当 初 我 的 女 朋 友 就 住 在 隔 壁 。
Back then my girlfriend lived next door.

137 当地　　　dāng dì　　**Noun:** local

dāng dì jū mín dōu zhī dào zhè jiàn shì
当 地 居 民 都 知 道 这 件 事 。
The **local** residents all know about this matter.

138 当然　　　dāng rán　　　**Adverb:** of course

wǒ dāng rán bù xiāng xìn tā de huà
我 当 然 不 相 信 他 的 话 。
Of course I don't believe his words.

139 当中　　　dāng zhōng　　　**Noun:** amongst

nǐ men dāng zhōng shéi bù xiāng xìn jiù qǐng jǔ shǒu
你 们 当 中 谁 不 相 信 ， 就 请 举 手 。
Whoever **amongst** you doesn't believe, then please raise your hands.

140 刀　　　dāo　　　**Noun:** knife

wǒ yǒu yì bǎ rì běn dāo hé yì bǎ zhōng guó jiàn
我 有 一 把 日 本 刀 和 一 把 中 国 剑 。
I have a Japanese **knife** and a Chinese sword.

141 导演　　　dǎo yǎn　　　**Noun:** director (movies)

tīng shuō zhè gè dǎo yǎn yǒu hěn duō qíng rén
听 说 这 个 导 演 有 很 多 情 人 。
I heard that this **director** has many mistresses.

142 到达　　　dào dá　　　**Verb:** to arrive

kè hù men gāng gāng dào dá bàn gōng shì le
客 户 们 刚 刚 到 达 办 公 室 了 。
The clients have just **arrived** at the office.

143 到底　　　dào dǐ　　　**Adverb:** on earth; exactly

nǐ de xīn lǐ dào dǐ zài xiǎng shén me
你 的 心 里 到 底 在 想 什 么 ？
What **on earth** are you thinking in your heart?

144 得分   dé fēn   **Verb:** to score

今 年 的 欧 洲 杯 ， 哪 个 球 队 **得 分**
jīn nián de ōu zhōu bēi   nǎ gè qiú duì dé fēn

最 高 ？
zuì gāo

This year's European Cup, which team **scored** the highest?

145 等待   děng dài   **Verb:** to wait for

难 民 们 在 **等 待** 政 府 的 救 援 。
nàn mín men zài děng dài zhèng fǔ de jiù yuán

Refugees are **waiting** for the government's rescue.

146 底下   dǐ xià   **Noun:** under; beneath

我 的 猫 和 狗 都 在 桌 子 **底 下** 。
wǒ de māo hé gǒu dōu zài zhuō zi dǐ xià

My cat and dog are both **under** the table.

147 地区   dì qū   **Noun:** region; area

每 个 国 家 都 有 贫 困 **地 区** 。
měi gè guó jiā dōu yǒu pín kùn dì qū

Every country has poor **areas**.

148 电视剧   diàn shì jù   **Noun:** TV series; television drama

你 最 喜 欢 的 **电 视 剧** 是 什 么 ？
nǐ zuì xǐ huān de diàn shì jù shì shén me

What is your favorite **TV drama**?

149 电视台   diàn shì tái   **Noun:** TV station

nǐ qù shì zhōng xīn cān guān guò diàn shì tái ma
你 去 市 中 心 参 观 过 **电 视 台** 吗 ？
Have you ever visited the **TV station** downtown?

150 电台   diàn tái   **Noun:** radio station

wǒ de wèi hūn qī zài diàn tái gōng zuò
我 的 未 婚 妻 在 **电 台** 工 作 。
My fiancée works in the **radio station**.

151 (电子)邮件   diàn zǐ yóu jiàn   **Noun:** email

tā měi tiān shōu dào zhì shǎo yī bǎi fēng yóu jiàn
她 每 天 收 到 至 少 一 百 封 **邮 件** 。
She receives at least one hundred **emails** a day.

152 调   diào   **Verb:** to transfer; to shift

tā zuì jìn bèi diào dào xiāng gǎng fēn bù le
她 最 近 被 **调** 到 香 港 分 部 了 。
She was recently **transferred** to the Hong Kong branch.

153 调查   diào chá   **Verb:** to investigate   **Noun:** investigation

Verb

jǐng chá qù shì gù xiàn chǎng diào chá le
警 察 去 事 故 现 场 **调 查** 了 。
The police went to the scene of the accident **to investigate**.

Noun

tīng shuō diào chá jié guǒ kuài chū lái le
听 说 ， **调 查** 结 果 快 出 来 了 。
I heard that the results of the **investigation** are coming out soon.

154 订   dìng   **Verb:** to order; to book

wǒ zài wǎng shàng dìng le jiǔ diàn fáng jiān
我 在 网 上 **订** 了 酒 店 房 间 。
I **booked** a hotel room online.

155 定期   dìng qī   **Adjective:** regular (fixed time)
Adverb: on a regular basis

Adj.
wǒ mā děi zuò dìng qī de shēn tǐ jiǎn chá
我 妈 得 做 **定 期** 的 身 体 检 查 。
My mother has to do **regular** physical examinations.

Adv.
fáng dōng yāo qiú dìng qī jiāo fáng zū
房 东 要 求 **定 期** 交 房 租 。
The landlord requires payments to be sent **on a regular basis**.

156 东部   dōng bù   **Noun:** east

wǒ de wèi hūn fū lái zì fǎ guó dōng bù
我 的 未 婚 夫 来 自 法 国 **东 部** 。
My fiancé is from the **east** of France.

157 动力   dòng lì   **Noun:** motivation

tā de ài shì wǒ zuì dà de dòng lì
她 的 爱 是 我 最 大 的 **动 力** 。
Her love is my greatest **motivation**.

158 动人   dòng rén   **Adjective:** moving; touching

zhè gè ài qíng gù shì fēi cháng dòng rén
这 个 爱 情 故 事 非 常 **动 人** 。
This love story is very **moving**.

159 读者　　dú zhě　　**Noun:** reader

zhè xiē dú zhě dōu shì tā de fěn sī
这 些 **读 者** 都 是 他 的 粉 丝 。
These **readers** are all his fans.

160 短处　　duǎn chù　　**Noun:** weakness; demerit

tā de cháng chù bǐ duǎn chù duō
他 的 长 处 比 **短 处** 多 。
He has more strengths than **weaknesses**.

161 短裤　　duǎn kù　　**Noun:** shorts

wǒ de yī guì lǐ yǒu liù tiáo bù tóng yán sè de
我 的 衣 柜 里 有 六 条 不 同 颜 色 的
duǎn kù
短 裤 。
I have six pairs of **shorts** of different colors in my closet.

162 短期　　duǎn qī　　**Noun:** short term

wǒ duǎn qī nèi bù dǎ suàn huàn gōng zuò
我 **短 期** 内 不 打 算 换 工 作 。
I don't plan to change jobs in the **short term**.

163 断　　duàn　　**Verb:** to break; to cut off

lí hūn hòu wǒ men jiù duàn le lián xì
离 婚 后 ， 我 们 就 **断** 了 联 系 。
After the divorce, we **cut off** contact.

164 队员　　duì yuán　　**Noun:** team member

wǒ de tuán duì yǒu jiǔ gè duì yuán
我 的 团 队 有 九 个 **队 员** 。
My team has nine **team members**.

165 对待　　duì dài　　**Verb:** to treat

tā men duì dài gōng zuò fēi cháng rèn zhēn
他 们 **对 待** 工 作 非 常 认 真 。
They **treat** their work very seriously.

166 对方　　duì fāng　　**Noun:** the other (side)

wǒ fāng hé duì fāng dōu yǒu shí gè xuǎn shǒu
我 方 和 **对 方** 都 有 十 个 选 手 。
Both our side and **the other side** have ten players.

167 对手　　duì shǒu　　**Noun:** opponent

jì zhù bú yào kàn dī nǐ de duì shǒu
记 住 ， 不 要 看 低 你 的 **对 手** 。
Remember, don't underestimate your **opponent**.

168 对象　　duì xiàng　　**Noun:** object; partner

nǐ men yán jiū de duì xiàng shì shén me
你 们 研 究 的 **对 象** 是 什 么 ？
What is the **object** of your research?

169 顿　　dùn　　**Classifier:** for meals

wǒ měi tiān chī sān dùn fàn nǐ ne
我 每 天 吃 三 **顿** 饭 ， 你 呢 ？
I eat three meals a day, how about you?

170 发表　　fā biǎo　　**Verb:** to publish

他在社交媒体上**发表**了反政府的言论。

He **published** anti-government remarks on social media.

171 发出　　fā chū　　**Verb:** to send out

所以，政府向他**发出**了警告。

So, the government **sent out** a warning to him.

172 发达　　fā dá　　**Adjective:** developed

发达城市有更多工作机会。

Developed cities have more job opportunities.

173 发动　　fā dòng　　**Verb:** to launch

有时候，强国对弱国**发动**战争。

Sometimes strong nations **launch** wars against weaker ones.

174 发明　　fā míng　　**Verb:** to invent
Noun: invention

Verb

是谁**发明**了原子弹？

Who **invented** the atomic bomb?

Noun

这是一个非常危险的**发明**。

This is a very dangerous **invention**.

175 发生　fā shēng　**Verb:** to happen

qǐng wèn, qián miàn fā shēng shén me le
请 问 ， 前 面 **发 生** 什 么 了 ？
Excuse me, what **happened** at the front?

176 发送　fā sòng　**Verb:** to send; to dispatch

wǎng shàng xiǎn shì, bāo guǒ yǐ jīng fā sòng le
网 上 显 示 ， 包 裹 已 经 **发 送** 了 。
It shows online that the package has been **dispatched**.

177 发言　fā yán　**Verb:** to speak out

zài huì yì shàng, lǎo bǎn gǔ lì dà jiā fā yán
在 会 议 上 ， 老 板 鼓 励 大 家 **发 言** 。
At the meeting, the boss encourages everyone **to speak out**.

178 发展　fā zhǎn　**Verb:** to develop　**Noun:** development

Verb
zuì jìn, quán qiú jīng jì fā zhǎn de hěn kuài
最 近 ， 全 球 经 济 **发 展** 得 很 快 。
Recently, the global economy has **developed** rapidly.

Noun
jīng jì fā zhǎn duì suǒ yǒu rén dōu hěn zhòng yào
经 济 **发 展** 对 所 有 人 都 很 重 要 。
Economic **development** is important to all people.

179 反对　fǎn duì　**Verb:** to oppose; to disapprove　**Noun:** disapproval

Verb
tīng shuō, yǒu rén fǎn duì tā men dìng hūn
听 说 ， 有 人 **反 对** 他 们 订 婚 。
I heard that some people **opposed** them getting engaged.

Noun
dàn shì, tā men bú zài hū tā de fǎn duì
但 是 ， 他 们 不 在 乎 他 的 **反 对** 。
However, they didn't care about his **disapproval**.

180 反复   fǎn fù   **Adverb:** keep; repeatedly

wǒ bà zǒng shì fǎn fù shuō tóng yí jù huà
我 爸 总 是 **反 复** 说 同 一 句 话 。
My dad **keeps** saying the same thing.

181 反应   fǎn yìng   **Verb:** to react
                                                Noun: reaction

Verb
tā dǎ lán qiú de shí hòu fǎn yìng de hěn kuài
他 打 篮 球 的 时 候 **反 应** 得 很 快 。
He **reacts** very quickly when he plays basketball.

Noun
tā duì nǐ de tū rán lí kāi shì shén me fǎn yìng
她 对 你 的 突 然 离 开 是 什 么 **反 应** ？
What was her **reaction** to your sudden departure?

182 反正   fǎn zhèng   **Adverb:** anyway

méi fǎn yìng fǎn zhèng tā bú zài hu
没 反 应 ， **反 正** 她 不 在 乎 ！
No reaction, she doesn't care **anyway**!

183 范围   fàn wéi   **Noun:** range

shēn qǐng dài kuǎn bù néng chāo chū zhè gè fàn wéi
申 请 贷 款 ， 不 能 超 出 这 个 **范 围** 。
Applying for a loan cannot exceed this **range**.

184 方式   fāng shì   **Noun:** style

nǐ xǐ huān shén me yàng de shēng huó fāng shì
你 喜 欢 什 么 样 的 生 活 **方 式** ？
What kind of life**style** do you like?

185 防   fáng   **Verb:** to guard against

<ruby>安<rt>ān</rt></ruby> <ruby>装<rt>zhuāng</rt></ruby> <ruby>监<rt>jiān</rt></ruby> <ruby>控<rt>kòng</rt></ruby> <ruby>是<rt>shì</rt></ruby> <ruby>为<rt>wèi</rt></ruby> <ruby>了<rt>le</rt></ruby> <ruby>防<rt>fáng</rt></ruby> <ruby>小<rt>xiǎo</rt></ruby> <ruby>偷<rt>tōu</rt></ruby> 。

Installing CCTV is to **guard against** thieves.

186 防止   fáng zhǐ   **Verb:** to prevent

<ruby>但<rt>dàn</rt></ruby> <ruby>是<rt>shì</rt></ruby> ， <ruby>这<rt>zhè</rt></ruby> <ruby>不<rt>bù</rt></ruby> <ruby>能<rt>néng</rt></ruby> <ruby>完<rt>wán</rt></ruby> <ruby>全<rt>quán</rt></ruby> <ruby>防<rt>fáng</rt></ruby> <ruby>止<rt>zhǐ</rt></ruby> <ruby>这<rt>zhè</rt></ruby> <ruby>种<rt>zhǒng</rt></ruby> <ruby>事<rt>shì</rt></ruby> <ruby>故<rt>gù</rt></ruby> 。

However, this cannot completely **prevent** such incidents.

187 房东   fáng dōng   **Noun:** landlord

<ruby>听<rt>tīng</rt></ruby> <ruby>说<rt>shuō</rt></ruby> ， <ruby>房<rt>fáng</rt></ruby> <ruby>东<rt>dōng</rt></ruby> <ruby>是<rt>shì</rt></ruby> <ruby>个<rt>gè</rt></ruby> <ruby>很<rt>hěn</rt></ruby> <ruby>有<rt>yǒu</rt></ruby> <ruby>钱<rt>qián</rt></ruby> <ruby>的<rt>de</rt></ruby> <ruby>胖<rt>pàng</rt></ruby> <ruby>子<rt>zi</rt></ruby> 。

I heard that the **landlord** is a very rich fat guy.

188 房屋   fáng wū   **Noun:** houses; tenement

<ruby>他<rt>tā</rt></ruby> <ruby>在<rt>zài</rt></ruby> <ruby>柏<rt>bó</rt></ruby> <ruby>林<rt>lín</rt></ruby> <ruby>有<rt>yǒu</rt></ruby> <ruby>四<rt>sì</rt></ruby> <ruby>套<rt>tào</rt></ruby> <ruby>房<rt>fáng</rt></ruby> <ruby>屋<rt>wū</rt></ruby> 。

He owns four **houses** in Berlin.

189 房租   fáng zū   **Noun:** rental payment

<ruby>我<rt>wǒ</rt></ruby> <ruby>每<rt>měi</rt></ruby> <ruby>个<rt>gè</rt></ruby> <ruby>月<rt>yuè</rt></ruby> <ruby>的<rt>de</rt></ruby> <ruby>房<rt>fáng</rt></ruby> <ruby>租<rt>zū</rt></ruby> <ruby>是<rt>shì</rt></ruby> <ruby>一<rt>yī</rt></ruby> <ruby>千<rt>qiān</rt></ruby> <ruby>欧<rt>ōu</rt></ruby> <ruby>元<rt>yuán</rt></ruby> 。

My monthly **rental payment** is one thousand euros.

190 访问　fǎng wèn

Verb: to visit (formal)
Noun: visit

Verb
fǎ guó zǒng tǒng xià gè yuè huì **fǎng wèn** yīng guó
法 国 总 统 下 个 月 会 **访 问** 英 国 。
The French president will **visit** the UK next month.

Noun
yīng guó shǒu xiàng hěn qī dài tā de **fǎng wèn**
英 国 首 相 很 期 待 他 的 **访 问** 。
The British Prime Minister is looking forward to his **visit**.

191 放到　fàng dào

Verb: to put;
to put into

qǐng bāng wǒ bǎ fàn cài **fàng dào** zhuō zi shàng
请 帮 我 把 饭 菜 **放 到** 桌 子 上 。
Please help me **put** the dishes on the table.

192 飞行　fēi xíng

Verb: to fly

diàn shì shàng chāo rén zài tiān shàng **fēi xíng**
电 视 上 ， 超 人 在 天 上 **飞 行** 。
On the TV, superman is **flying** in the sky.

193 费　fèi

Noun: fee; expense

tīng shuō lún dūn de shēng huó **fèi** hěn gāo
听 说 ， 伦 敦 的 生 活 **费** 很 高 。
I heard that the living **expense** in London is very high.

nǐ dǎ suàn gěi tā duō shǎo xiǎo **fèi**
你 打 算 给 他 多 少 小 **费** ？
How much tip (small **fee**) do you plan to give him?

194 费用　fèi yòng

Noun: cost; outlay

duō shù rén bù néng chéng dān zhè yàng gāo de **fèi yòng**
多 数 人 不 能 承 担 这 样 高 的 **费 用** 。
Most people cannot afford such a high **cost**.

195 分别　fēn bié

Verb: to part
Adverb: respectively; individually

Verb

tā hé tài tai yǐ jīng fēn bié bàn nián le
他 和 太 太 已 经 **分 别** 半 年 了 。
He and his wife have **parted** for half a year.

Adv.

tā zài gěi gù kè fēn bié jiè shào zhè xiē chǎn pǐn
他 在 给 顾 客 **分 别** 介 绍 这 些 产 品 。
He is introducing these products to customers **respectively**.

196 分配　fēn pèi

Verb: to distribute
Noun: distribution

Verb

zhǔ guǎn gěi wǒ men fēn pèi le rèn wù
主 管 给 我 们 **分 配** 了 任 务 。
The director **distributed** tasks to us.

Noun

yǒu rén jué de zhè gè fēn pèi bù gōng píng
有 人 觉 得 这 个 **分 配** 不 公 平 。
Some people feel that this **distribution** is unfair.

197 分组　fēn zǔ

Verb: to group

fēn zǔ tǎo lùn fēi cháng yǒu xiào
分 组 讨 论 非 常 有 效 。
Grouping discussions is very effective.

198 丰富　fēng fù

Adjective: abundant

zhè kuài bǎo dì de zī yuán hěn fēng fù
这 块 宝 地 的 资 源 很 **丰 富** 。
This treasure land is **abundant** in resources.

199 风险　fēng xiǎn

Noun: risk

nǐ dān xīn tóu zī fēng xiǎn ma
你 担 心 投 资 **风 险** 吗 ？
Are you worried about investment **risks**?

200 否定   fǒu dìng   **Verb:** to refute; to negate
Adjective: negative

Verb

zhè gè lǐ lùn bèi kē xué jiā men fǒu dìng le
这 个 理 论 被 科 学 家 们 **否 定** 了 。
This theory has been **refuted** by scientists.

Adj.

tā men dōu gěi le fǒu dìng de huí dá
他 们 都 给 了 **否 定** 的 回 答 。
They all gave **negative** answers.

201 否认   fǒu rèn   **Verb:** to repudiate; to deny

zhè gè fàn rén méi yǒu fǒu rèn tā de zuì xíng
这 个 犯 人 没 有 **否 认** 他 的 罪 行 。
The prisoner did not **deny** his crime.

202 服装   fú zhuāng   **Noun:** clothing

wǒ de guī mì gāng gāng kāi le yì jiā fú zhuāng diàn
我 的 闺 蜜 刚 刚 开 了 一 家 **服 装** 店 。
My best friend just opened a **clothing** store.

203 福   fú   **Noun:** blessing; good fortune

tā bù zhī dào zhè shì fú hái shì huò
她 不 知 道 这 是 **福** 还 是 祸 。
She doesn't know whether it is a **blessing** or a curse.

204 父母   fù mǔ   **Noun:** parents; father and mother

tīng shuō tā fù mǔ gěi tā mǎi le yí liàng fǎ
听 说 ， 他 **父 母** 给 他 买 了 一 辆 法
lā lì
拉 利 。
I heard that his **parents** bought him a Ferrari.

205 父亲   fù qīn   **Noun:** father

毕 竟 ， 他 父 亲 是 亿 万 富 翁 。
bì jìng tā fù qīn shì yì wàn fù wēng

After all, his **father** is a billionaire.

206 付   fù   **Verb:** to pay

请 问 ， 可 以 用 信 用 卡 付 款 吗 ？
qǐng wèn kě yǐ yòng xìn yòng kǎ fù kuǎn ma

Excuse me, can I **pay** (money) by credit card?

207 负责   fù zé   **Verb:** to be in charge; to be responsible for

你 知 道 是 谁 负 责 这 个 项 目 吗 ？
nǐ zhī dào shì shéi fù zé zhè gè xiàng mù ma

Do you know who is **in charge** of this project?

208 复印   fù yìn   **Verb:** to photocopy

麻 烦 你 帮 我 复 印 一 下 护 照 。
má fán nǐ bāng wǒ fù yìn yí xià hù zhào

May I trouble you to make a **photocopy** of my passport?

209 复杂   fù zá   **Adjective:** complex; complicated

他 跟 他 前 女 友 的 关 系 很 复 杂 。
tā gēn tā qián nǚ yǒu de guān xi hěn fù zá

His relationship with his ex-girlfriend is **complicated**.

210 富   fù   **Adjective:** rich; wealthy

其 实 ， 富 人 和 穷 人 的 思 维 不 一 样 。
qí shí fù rén hé qióng rén de sī wéi bù yí yàng

In fact, **rich** people and poor people have different mindsets.

211 改进　　gǎi jìn

Verb: to improve (make better)
Noun: improvement

Verb
我 们 要 想 办 法 改 进 这 个 软 件 。
wǒ men yào xiǎng bàn fǎ gǎi jìn zhè gè ruǎn jiàn
We have to find ways to **improve** this software.

Noun
客 户 对 这 个 改 进 很 满 意 。
kè hù duì zhè gè gǎi jìn hěn mǎn yì
Customers are very happy with this **improvement**.

212 改造　　gǎi zào

Verb: to transform
Noun: transformation

Verb
我 打 算 在 暑 假 改 造 我 的 花 园 。
wǒ dǎ suàn zài shǔ jià gǎi zào wǒ de huā yuán
I'm going **to transform** my garden for the summer holiday.

Noun
改 造 费 用 大 概 是 两 千 美 元 。
gǎi zào fèi yòng dà gài shì liǎng qiān měi yuán
The **transformation** cost is about $2,000.

213 概念　　gài niàn

Noun: concept

你 可 以 解 释 这 个 概 念 吗 ？
nǐ kě yǐ jiě shì zhè gè gài niàn ma
Can you explain this **concept**?

214 赶　　gǎn

Verb: to rush; to hurry

我 在 赶 时 间 上 班 ， 不 能 多 聊 。
wǒ zài gǎn shí jiān shàng bān bù néng duō liáo
I'm **rushing** (time) for work and can't talk much.

215 赶到　　gǎn dào

Verb: to manage to arrive (hurriedly)

他 赶 到 的 时 候 ， 奶 奶 已 经 去 世 了 。
tā gǎn dào de shí hòu nǎi nai yǐ jīng qù shì le
When he **managed to arrive**, grandma had passed away.

216 赶紧   gǎn jǐn   **Adverb:** quickly; hurriedly

tā hěn shāng xīn，nǐ gǎn jǐn qù ān wèi tā

他 很 伤 心 ， 你 **赶 紧** 去 安 慰 他 。

He is very sad, go **quickly** to comfort him.

217 赶快   gǎn kuài   be quick; hurry up

gǎn kuài！bù rán wǒ men huì chí dào

赶 快 ！ 不 然 我 们 会 迟 到 。

Hurry up! Otherwise we will be late.

218 敢   gǎn   **Verb:** to dare

tā huì gōng fu，méi rén gǎn qī fù tā

他 会 功 夫 ， 没 人 **敢** 欺 负 他 。

He knows kung fu, no one **dares** to bully him.

219 感冒   gǎn mào   **Noun:** cold (illness)

wǒ dé gǎn mào le， bí zi hé yǎn jīng dōu bù shū fu

我 得 **感 冒** 了 ， 鼻 子 和 眼 睛 都 不 舒 服 。

I have a **cold** and my nose and eyes are both uncomfortable.

220 感情   gǎn qíng   **Noun:** relationship; emotion

tā men jié hūn shí nián le， gǎn qíng hěn wěn dìng

他 们 结 婚 十 年 了 ， **感 情** 很 稳 定 。

They have been married for ten years and their **relationship** is very stable.

zài yǒu xiē chǎng hé， yí dìng yào kòng zhì gè rén gǎn qíng

在 有 些 场 合 ， 一 定 要 控 制 个 人 **感 情** 。

On some occasions, one must control personal **emotions**.

221 感受　　gǎn shòu　　**Noun:** feeling

wǒ dāng rán zài hū nǐ de gǎn shòu
我 当 然 在 乎 你 的 感 受 。
Of course I care about your **feelings**.

222 干吗　　gàn má　　**Interrogative:** why (colloquial)

nǐ gàn má bù tí qián gào sù wǒ
你 干 吗 不 提 前 告 诉 我 ？
Why didn't you tell me in advance?

223 高速　　gāo sù　　**Noun:** high speed

zhè tiáo lù jìn zhǐ gāo sù xíng shǐ
这 条 路 禁 止 高 速 行 驶 。
High speed driving is prohibited on this road.

224 高速公路　　gāo sù gōng lù　　**Noun:** expressway

tīng shuō zhè tiáo gāo sù gōng lù cháng cháng dǔ chē
听 说 ， 这 条 高 速 公 路 常 常 堵 车 。
I heard that this **expressway** is often jammed.

225 告别　　gào bié　　**Verb:** to bid farewell　**Noun:** farewell

Verb
lǎo bǎn tuì xiū le yào qù gēn yuán gōng men gào bié
老 板 退 休 了 ， 要 去 跟 员 工 们 告 别 。
The boss has retired and wants to **say farewell** to the employees.

Noun
wǒ yě huì cān jiā zhè gè gào bié wǎn huì
我 也 会 参 加 这 个 告 别 晚 会 。
I will also attend this **farewell** party.

226 歌迷   gē mí   **Noun:** fan (of singers)

wǒ men dōu shì liú xíng gē wáng de gē mí
我 们 都 是 流 行 歌 王 的 **歌 迷** 。
We are all **fans** of the King of Pop.

227 歌声   gē shēng   **Noun:** singing (voice)

tā de gē shēng yòu wēn róu yòu hǎo tīng
他 的 **歌 声** 又 温 柔 又 好 听 。
His **singing voice** is soft and pleasant.

228 歌手   gē shǒu   **Noun:** singer; vocalist

tā shì quán shì jiè zuì bàng de gē shǒu
他 是 全 世 界 最 棒 的 **歌 手** ！
He is the best **singer** in the world!

229 个人   gè rén   **Adjective:** personal
                                             Noun: individual

Adj.   zhè shì tā de gè rén yǐn sī
这 是 他 的 **个 人** 隐 私 。
This is his **personal** privacy.

Noun   rèn hé gè rén dōu yīng gāi biǎo shì zūn zhòng
任 何 **个 人** 都 应 该 表 示 尊 重 。
Any **individual** should show respect.

230 个性   gè xìng   **Noun:** personality

nǐ zhēn de liǎo jiě tā de gè xìng ma
你 真 的 了 解 她 的 **个 性** 吗 ？
Do you really understand her **personality**?

231 各　　　　　gè　　　　　**Adverb:** variously; respectively (each)

wǒ men měi gè rén dōu gè yǒu yōu diǎn hé quē diǎn
我 们 每 个 人 都 **各** 有 优 点 和 缺 点 。
Each of us has strengths and weaknesses **respectively**.

232 各地　　　　gè dì　　　　**Noun:** various regions; everywhere; all over

wǒ men jù lè bù de chéng yuán lái zì quán guó gè dì
我 们 俱 乐 部 的 成 员 来 自 全 国 **各 地** 。
Members of our club come from **all over** the country.

233 各位　　　　gè wèi　　　　**Noun:** everybody

gè wèi wǒ men yì qǐ jǔ bēi gān bēi
各 位 ， 我 们 一 起 举 杯 ， 干 杯 ！
Everybody, let's raise our glasses together, cheers!

234 各种　　　　gè zhǒng　　　　**Noun:** all kinds; various; every kind

wǒ mǎi le gè zhǒng yán sè de qì qiú
我 买 了 **各 种** 颜 色 的 气 球 。
I bought balloons of **various** colors.

235 各自　　　　gè zì　　　　**Noun:** each

bǐ sài mǎ shàng kāi shǐ qǐng gè zì zhǔn bèi
比 赛 马 上 开 始 ， 请 **各 自** 准 备 ！
The game is about to start, please (**each** of you) get ready!

236 根本　　　　gēn běn　　　　**Adverb:** at all

kě shi tā gēn běn bù dǒng bǐ sài guī zé
可 是 ， 他 **根 本** 不 懂 比 赛 规 则 ！
However, he doesn't understand the rules of the game **at all**!

237 更(加)   gèng jiā   **Adverb:** more; even more

nǐ yīng gāi duì tā gēng jiā nài xīn
你 应 该 对 他 **更 加** 耐 心 。
You should be **more** patient with him.

238 工厂   gōng chǎng   **Noun:** factory

tīng shuō nà gè gōng chǎng qù nián dǎo bì le
听 说 ， 那 个 **工 厂** 去 年 倒 闭 了 。
I heard that the **factory** closed down last year.

239 工程师   gōng chéng shī   **Noun:** engineer

wǒ de wèi hūn fū shì diàn nǎo gōng chéng shī
我 的 未 婚 夫 是 电 脑 **工 程 师** 。
My fiancé is a computer **engineer**.

240 工夫   gōng fu   **Noun:** time or effort (colloquial)

nǐ jué de zuò jiān bǐng huā gōng fu ma
你 觉 得 做 煎 饼 花 **工 夫** 吗 ？
Do you think it takes **time** to make pancakes?

241 工具   gōng jù   **Noun:** tool

wǒ de gōng jù diū le bāng wǒ zhǎo yi zhǎo
我 的 **工 具** 丢 了 ， 帮 我 找 一 找 。
My **tool** is lost, help me find it.

242 工业   gōng yè   **Noun:** industry

tā de dà xué zhuān yè shì gōng yè guǎn lǐ
他 的 大 学 专 业 是 **工 业** 管 理 。
His college major was **Industrial** Management.

243 工资   gōng zī   **Noun:** wages; salary

wǒ de gōng zī yì bān bú suàn gāo
我 的 **工 资** 一 般 ， 不 算 高 。
My **salary** is average, not considered high.

244 公布   gōng bù   **Verb:** to publish; to announce
Noun: announcement

Verb
tā men gāng gāng gōng bù le lí hūn de xiāo xī
他 们 刚 刚 **公 布** 了 离 婚 的 消 息 。
They just **announced** the news of their divorce.

Noun
tīng shuō shì lǜ shī bāng tā men fā de gōng bù
听 说 ， 是 律 师 帮 他 们 发 的 **公 布** 。
I heard that it was the lawyer who made the **announcement** for them.

245 公共   gōng gòng   **Noun:** public

zài gōng gòng chǎng suǒ dǎ jià shì wéi fǎ de
在 **公 共** 场 所 打 架 是 违 法 的 。
It is illegal to fight in **public** places.

246 公开   gōng kāi   **Verb:** to disclose; to open

tā zài shè jiāo méi tǐ shàng gōng kāi le dào qiàn xìn
他 在 社 交 媒 体 上 **公 开** 了 道 歉 信 。
He **disclosed** the apology letter on social media.

247 公民   gōng mín   **Noun:** citizen

zhèng fǔ yīng gāi bǎo hù gōng mín de hé fǎ quán
政 府 应 该 保 护 **公 民** 的 合 法 权 。
The government should protect the legitimate rights of **citizens**.

248 公务员   gōng wù yuán   **Noun:** civil servant; public functionary

wǒ de wèi hūn qī shì gōng wù yuán
我 的 未 婚 妻 是 **公 务 员** 。
My fiancée is a **civil servant**.

249 功夫   gōng fu   **Noun:** kung fu

tā zuì xǐ huān de gōng fu míng xīng shì lǐ xiǎo lóng
她 最 喜 欢 的 **功 夫** 明 星 是 李 小 龙 。
Her favorite **kung fu** star is Bruce Lee.

250 功课   gōng kè   **Noun:** homework; schoolwork

wǒ de zhí nǚ tǎo yàn zuò shù xué gōng kè
我 的 侄 女 讨 厌 做 数 学 **功 课** 。
My niece dislikes doing math **homework**.

251 功能   gōng néng   **Noun:** function

zhì néng shǒu jī de gōng néng yuè lái yuè duō
智 能 手 机 的 **功 能** 越 来 越 多 。
Smartphones have more and more **functions**.

252 共同   gòng tóng   **Adjective:** common; mutual

wǒ de ér zi hé zhí zi yǒu hěn duō gòng tóng ài hào
我 的 儿 子 和 侄 子 有 很 多 **共 同** 爱 好 。
My son and nephew share many **common** hobbies.

253 共有   gòng yǒu   **Verb:** to share; to have altogether

wǒ de shuāng bāo tāi nǚ ér gòng yǒu yí gè fáng jiān
我 的 双 胞 胎 女 儿 **共 有** 一 个 房 间 。
My twin daughters **share** a room.

254 姑娘   gū niang   **Noun:** young woman

tā nián qīng de shí hòu ài guò yí gè rì běn gū niang
他 年 轻 的 时 候 爱 过 一 个 日 本 **姑 娘** 。
When he was young, he loved a Japanese **young woman**.

255 古   gǔ   **Adjective:** ancient

wǒ hé tā dōu xǐ huān dú gǔ shī
我 和 她 都 喜 欢 读 **古** 诗 。
Both she and I like to read **ancient** poems.

256 古代   gǔ dài   **Noun:** ancient (time)

kǒng zǐ shì zhōng guó gǔ dài de jiào yù jiā
孔 子 是 中 国 **古 代** 的 教 育 家 。
Confucius was an educator in **ancient** China.

257 故乡   gù xiāng   **Noun:** hometown

tā de gù xiāng zài tài guó nán bù
他 的 **故 乡** 在 泰 国 南 部 。
His **hometown** is in southern Thailand.

258 挂   guà   **Verb:** to hang

wǒ de shū fáng guà le yí fú zhōng guó shān shuǐ huà
我 的 书 房 **挂** 了 一 幅 中 国 山 水 画 。
I **hung** a Chinese landscape painting in my study room.

259 关系   guān xi   **Noun:** relationship; connection

wǒ hé fù mǔ de guān xi yì zhí hěn hǎo
我 和 父 母 的 **关 系** 一 直 很 好 。
My **relationship** with my parents has always been good.

260 关注   guān zhù   **Verb:** to pay attention to (show interest)
Noun: attention

Verb
^{fěn} ^{sī} ^{men} ^{hěn} ^{guān} ^{zhù} ^{tā} ^{de} ^{sī} ^{shēng} ^{huó}
粉 丝 们 很 **关 注** 他 的 私 生 活 。
Fans really **pay attention to** his private life.

Noun
^{zhè} ^{zhǒng} ^{guān} ^{zhù} ^{ràng} ^{tā} ^{gǎn} ^{jué} ^{yā} ^{lì} ^{hěn} ^{dà}
这 种 **关 注** 让 他 感 觉 压 力 很 大 。
This kind of **attention** made him feel a lot of pressure.

261 观察   guān chá   **Verb:** to observe
Noun: observation

Verb
^{tā} ^{shàn} ^{cháng} ^{guān} ^{chá} ^{bié} ^{rén} ^{de} ^{zhī} ^{tǐ} ^{yǔ} ^{yán}
他 擅 长 **观 察** 别 人 的 肢 体 语 言 。
He is good at **observing** other people's body language.

Noun
^{tā} ^{de} ^{jié} ^{lùn} ^{shì} ^{lái} ^{zì} ^{zǐ} ^{xi} ^{de} ^{guān} ^{chá}
他 的 结 论 是 来 自 仔 细 的 **观 察** 。
His conclusions come from careful **observation**.

262 观看   guān kàn   **Verb:** to watch (shows)

^{wǒ} ^{men} ^{xià} ^{zhōu} ^{mò} ^{yào} ^{yì} ^{qǐ} ^{guān} ^{kàn} ^{bā} ^{lěi} ^{wǔ}
我 们 下 周 末 要 一 起 **观 看** 芭 蕾 舞
^{biǎo} ^{yǎn}
表 演 。
We're going to **watch** a ballet show together next weekend.

263 观念   guān niàn   **Noun:** views; values

^{shàng} ^{yí} ^{dài} ^{de} ^{rén} ^{guān} ^{niàn} ^{bǐ} ^{wǒ} ^{men} ^{de} ^{gèng} ^{bǎo} ^{shǒu}
上 一 代 的 人 **观 念** 比 我 们 的 更 保 守 。
The previous generation had more conservative **views** than ours.

264 观众   guān zhòng   **Noun: audience**

<ruby>听<rt>tīng</rt></ruby> <ruby>说<rt>shuō</rt></ruby>，<ruby>那<rt>nà</rt></ruby> <ruby>些<rt>xiē</rt></ruby> <ruby>观<rt>guān</rt></ruby> <ruby>众<rt>zhòng</rt></ruby> <ruby>来<rt>lái</rt></ruby> <ruby>自<rt>zì</rt></ruby> <ruby>世<rt>shì</rt></ruby> <ruby>界<rt>jiè</rt></ruby> <ruby>各<rt>gè</rt></ruby> <ruby>地<rt>dì</rt></ruby>。
I heard that those **audiences** came from all over the world.

265 管   guǎn   **Verb: to control; to deal with**

<ruby>很<rt>hěn</rt></ruby> <ruby>多<rt>duō</rt></ruby> <ruby>家<rt>jiā</rt></ruby> <ruby>长<rt>zhǎng</rt></ruby> <ruby>觉<rt>jué</rt></ruby> <ruby>得<rt>de</rt></ruby> <ruby>管<rt>guǎn</rt></ruby> <ruby>孩<rt>hái</rt></ruby> <ruby>子<rt>zi</rt></ruby> <ruby>很<rt>hěn</rt></ruby> <ruby>难<rt>nán</rt></ruby>。
Many parents find it difficult **to deal with** kids.

266 管理   guǎn lǐ   **Verb: to manage**
Noun: management

Verb
<ruby>老<rt>lǎo</rt></ruby> <ruby>板<rt>bǎn</rt></ruby> <ruby>说<rt>shuō</rt></ruby> <ruby>管<rt>guǎn</rt></ruby> <ruby>理<rt>lǐ</rt></ruby> <ruby>公<rt>gōng</rt></ruby> <ruby>司<rt>sī</rt></ruby> <ruby>不<rt>bù</rt></ruby> <ruby>容<rt>róng</rt></ruby> <ruby>易<rt>yì</rt></ruby>。
The boss said that **managing** the company is not easy.

Noun
<ruby>他<rt>tā</rt></ruby> <ruby>在<rt>zài</rt></ruby> <ruby>学<rt>xué</rt></ruby> <ruby>习<rt>xí</rt></ruby> <ruby>如<rt>rú</rt></ruby> <ruby>何<rt>hé</rt></ruby> <ruby>改<rt>gǎi</rt></ruby> <ruby>善<rt>shàn</rt></ruby> <ruby>管<rt>guǎn</rt></ruby> <ruby>理<rt>lǐ</rt></ruby> <ruby>方<rt>fāng</rt></ruby> <ruby>式<rt>shì</rt></ruby>。
He is learning how to improve his **management** style.

267 光   guāng   **Noun: light**
Adverb: merely; just

Noun
<ruby>房<rt>fáng</rt></ruby> <ruby>间<rt>jiān</rt></ruby> <ruby>的<rt>de</rt></ruby> <ruby>灯<rt>dēng</rt></ruby> <ruby>光<rt>guāng</rt></ruby> <ruby>太<rt>tài</rt></ruby> <ruby>暗<rt>àn</rt></ruby> <ruby>了<rt>le</rt></ruby>，<ruby>不<rt>bú</rt></ruby> <ruby>适<rt>shì</rt></ruby> <ruby>合<rt>hé</rt></ruby> <ruby>看<rt>kàn</rt></ruby> <ruby>书<rt>shū</rt></ruby>。
The lamp (**light**) in the room is too dim, not suitable for reading.

Adv.
<ruby>要<rt>yào</rt></ruby> <ruby>成<rt>chéng</rt></ruby> <ruby>功<rt>gōng</rt></ruby>，<ruby>光<rt>guāng</rt></ruby> <ruby>努<rt>nǔ</rt></ruby> <ruby>力<rt>lì</rt></ruby> <ruby>还<rt>hái</rt></ruby> <ruby>不<rt>bú</rt></ruby> <ruby>够<rt>gòu</rt></ruby>！
To succeed, **merely** hard working is not enough!

268 光明   guāng míng   **Noun: light (poetic)**

<ruby>伟<rt>wěi</rt></ruby> <ruby>大<rt>dà</rt></ruby> <ruby>的<rt>de</rt></ruby> <ruby>领<rt>lǐng</rt></ruby> <ruby>袖<rt>xiù</rt></ruby> <ruby>是<rt>shì</rt></ruby> <ruby>国<rt>guó</rt></ruby> <ruby>家<rt>jiā</rt></ruby> <ruby>的<rt>de</rt></ruby> <ruby>光<rt>guāng</rt></ruby> <ruby>明<rt>míng</rt></ruby>。
A great leader is the **light** of the country.

269 广播　　guǎng bō　　**Noun:** broadcast

wǒ péng yǒu zài yīng guó guǎng bō gōng sī shàng bān
我 朋 友 在 英 国 **广 播** 公 司 上 班 。
My friend works for the BBC (British **Broadcasting** Corporation).

270 广大　　guǎng dà　　**Adjective:** vast

zhè gè jī gòu de yè wù fàn wéi guǎng dà
这 个 机 构 的 业 务 范 围 **广 大** 。
The scope of the agency's business is **vast**.

271 规定　　guī dìng　　**Verb:** to stipulate
　　　　　　　　　　　　　　　Noun: regulation

Verb
gōng sī guī dìng yuán gōng kě yǐ xuǎn zé zài jiā shàng bān
公 司 **规 定** 员 工 可 以 选 择 在 家 上 班 。
The company **stipulates** that employees can choose to work from home.

Noun
zhè gè guī dìng hěn shòu dà jiā huān yíng
这 个 **规 定** 很 受 大 家 欢 迎 。
This **regulation** is very well received by everyone.

272 规范　　guī fàn　　**Noun:** criterion; rule; code

xué xiào zài kǎo lù gǎi xiě xué shēng de xíng wéi guī fàn
学 校 在 考 虑 改 写 学 生 的 行 为 **规 范** 。
The school is considering rewriting student **code** of conduct.

273 国内　　guó nèi　　**Noun:** domestic

zhè gè jǐng diǎn xī yǐn le hěn duō guó nèi hé guó
这 个 景 点 吸 引 了 很 多 **国 内** 和 国
wài de yóu kè
外 的 游 客 。
This scenic spot attracts many **domestic** and foreign tourists.

53

274 国庆　　guó qìng　　**Noun:** National Day

zhōng guó de guó qìng jié shì shí yuè yī hào
中 国 的 国 庆 节 是 十 月 一 号 。
China's **National Day** (festival) is October 1st.

275 果然　　guǒ rán　　**Adverb:** surely; sure enough

zhè gè mó tè guǒ rán gōu xìng gǎn
这 个 模 特 果 然 够 性 感 ！
This model is **surely** sexy enough!

276 果汁　　guǒ zhī　　**Noun:** fruit juice

yī shēng jiàn yì tā duō hē guǒ zhī
医 生 建 议 他 多 喝 果 汁 。
The doctor advised him to drink more **fruit juice**.

277 过程　　guò chéng　　**Noun:** process; procedure

zhè běn xiàng cè jì lù le wǒ men de liàn ài guò chéng
这 本 相 册 记 录 了 我 们 的 恋 爱 过 程 。
This photo album records our love **process**.

278 过去　　guò qù　　**Verb:** to go over
Noun: past; foretime

Verb
cóng zhè guò qù dà gài yào shí fēn zhōng
从 这 过 去 ， 大 概 要 十 分 钟 。
Going over from here will take about ten minutes.

Noun
guò qù bú zhòng yào zhòng yào de shì xiàn zài hé jiāng lái
过 去 不 重 要 ， 重 要 的 是 现 在 和 将 来 。
The **past** is not important, what matters is the present and the future.

279 哈哈   hā ha   **Interjection:** ha-ha

hā ha   wǒ gāng gāng yù dào le yí gè chāo jí bèn dàn
哈 哈！我 刚 刚 遇 到 了 一 个 超 级 笨 蛋！
Ha ha! I just met a super idiot!

280 海关   hǎi guān   **Noun:** customs

hǎi guān yāo qiú wǒ men chū shì hù zhào hé qiān zhèng
海 关 要 求 我 们 出 示 护 照 和 签 证。
Customs asked us to show our passports and visas.

281 害怕   hài pà   **Verb:** to be afraid; to fear

bié hài pà ， zhè zhǐ shì yí gè mèng
别 害 怕， 这 只 是 一 个 梦。
Don't **be afraid**, it's just a dream.

282 行   háng   **Noun:** row; line

zhè yì háng zì xiě de hěn piào liang
这 一 行 字 写 得 很 漂 亮。
This **line** of characters is written very beautifully.

283 好好   hǎo hǎo   **Adverb:** good; well (colloquial)

zài jiàn ！ jì de yào hǎo hǎo zhào gù zì jǐ
再 见！ 记 得 要 好 好 照 顾 自 己。
Goodbye! Remember to take **good** care of yourself.

284 好奇   hào qí   **Adjective:** curious

wǒ hěn hào qí tā men wèi shén me fēn jū
我 很 好 奇 他 们 为 什 么 分 居。
I'm **curious** why they are separated.

285 合 　　　　hé 　　　**Verb:** to suit; to match

chuān cài hěn hé wǒ de wèi kǒu
川 菜 很 **合** 我 的 胃 口 。
Sichuan cuisine **suits** my taste.

286 合法 　　　　hé fǎ 　　　**Adjective:** legal

zài zhōng guó ， xī dú bú shì hé fǎ de ， ér shì
在 中 国 ， 吸 毒 不 是 **合 法** 的 ， 而 是
wéi fǎ de
违 法 的 。
In China, taking drugs is not **legal**, but illegal.

287 合格 　　　　hé gé 　　　**Adjective:** qualified

wǒ men yí gòng yǒu sān míng hé gé de miàn shì zhě
我 们 一 共 有 三 名 **合 格** 的 面 试 者 。
In total we have three **qualified** interviewees.

288 合理 　　　　hé lǐ 　　　**Adjective:** reasonable

wǒ jué de tā men de gōng zī yāo qiú hěn hé lǐ
我 觉 得 他 们 的 工 资 要 求 很 **合 理** 。
I think their salary demands are very **reasonable**.

289 合作 　　　　hé zuò 　　　**Verb:** to cooperate
　　　　　　　　　　　　　　　　　Noun: cooperation

Verb
nǐ dǎ suàn gēn tā de gōng sī hé zuò ma
你 打 算 跟 他 的 公 司 **合 作** 吗 ？
Are you going to **cooperate** with his company?

Noun
wǒ zhù nǐ men hé zuò shùn lì
我 祝 你 们 **合 作** 顺 利 ！
I wish you a smooth **cooperation**!

290 和平   hé píng   **Noun:** peace

lián hé guó de rèn wù shì wéi hù shì jiè hé píng
联 合 国 的 任 务 是 维 护 世 界 **和 平** 。
The mission of the United Nations is to keep world **peace.**

291 红茶   hóng chá   **Noun:** red tea

wǒ měi tiān zǎo shàng qǐ chuáng hòu huì hē yì bēi hóng chá
我 每 天 早 上 起 床 后 会 喝 一 杯 **红 茶** 。
I drink a cup of **red tea** every morning when I wake up.

292 红酒   hóng jiǔ   **Noun:** red wine

wǒ měi tiān wǎn shàng shuì jiào qián huì hē yì bēi hóng jiǔ
我 每 天 晚 上 睡 觉 前 会 喝 一 杯 **红 酒** 。
I drink a glass of **red wine** every night before I sleep.

293 后果   hòu guǒ   **Noun:** consequence

jiǔ jià de hòu guǒ fēi cháng yán zhòng
酒 驾 的 **后 果** 非 常 严 重 。
The **consequences** of drink-driving are very severe.

294 后面   hòu miàn   **Noun:** behind

xiǎo xīn nǐ de chē zi hòu miàn yǒu yì tiáo gǒu
小 心 ， 你 的 车 子 **后 面** 有 一 条 狗 。
Be careful, there is a dog **behind** your car.

295 后年   hòu nián   **Noun:** the year after next

wǒ hòu nián huì qù mǎ lái xī yà lǚ yóu
我 **后 年** 会 去 马 来 西 亚 旅 游 。
I will travel to Malaysia **the year after next.**

296 互联网　　hù lián wǎng　　**Noun:** Internet

zhè xiē hù lián wǎng zhuān jiā lái zì yìn dù
这 些 **互 联 网** 专 家 来 自 印 度 。
These **Internet** experts are from India.

297 互相　　hù xiāng　　**Adverb:** each other

hǎo péng yǒu dāng rán yīng gāi hù xiāng bāng zhù
好 朋 友 当 然 应 该 **互 相** 帮 助 。
Good friends should of course help **each other**.

298 划船　　huá chuán　　**Verb:** to row (a boat)

wǒ bà cóng xiǎo jiù hěn shàn cháng huá chuán
我 爸 从 小 就 很 擅 长 **划 船** 。
My dad has been good at **rowing boats** since he was a child.

299 华人　　huá rén　　**Noun:** overseas Chinese

duō shù de huá rén dōu huì shuō huá yǔ
多 数 的 **华 人** 都 会 说 华 语 。
Most **overseas Chinese** can speak Chinese (language).

300 化　　huà　　**Suffix:** indicate transformation (adj. + 化)

wǒ yào měi huà kè tīng yě yào lǜ huà huā yuán
我 要 **美 化** 客 厅 ， 也 要 **绿 化** 花 园 。
I want to **beautify** the living room, and **greenify** the garden.

301 话剧　　huà jù　　**Noun:** stage play

wǒ men míng wǎn qù kàn huà jù biǎo yǎn zěn me yàng
我 们 明 晚 去 看 **话 剧** 表 演 ， 怎 么 样 ？
How about we go to watch a **stage play** tomorrow night?

302 话题   huà tí   **Noun:** topic (conversation)

wǒ bù xiǎng tǎo lùn zhè gè huà tí
我 不 想 讨 论 这 个 **话 题** 。
I don't want to discuss this **topic**.

303 欢乐   huān lè   **Adjective:** joyful
Noun: joy

Adj.
xīn nián de qì fēn hěn huān lè
新 年 的 气 氛 很 **欢 乐** 。
The New Year's atmosphere is very **joyful**.

Noun
měi gè rén dōu yǒu huān lè hé bēi shāng
每 个 人 都 有 **欢 乐** 和 悲 伤 。
Everyone has **joys** and sorrows.

304 环   huán   **Noun:** ring; loop

tā zài běi jīng sān huán lù mǎi le xīn fáng zi
她 在 北 京 三 **环** 路 买 了 新 房 子 。
She bought a new house on Beijing's Third **Ring** Road.

305 环保   huán bǎo   **Noun:** environmental protection

hěn duō rén jiā rù le tā men de huán bǎo huó dòng
很 多 人 加 入 了 他 们 的 **环 保** 活 动 。
Many people joined their **environmental protection** activities.

306 环境   huán jìng   **Noun:** environment

dà jiā dōu jué de bǎo hù huán jìng hěn zhòng yào
大 家 都 觉 得 保 护 **环 境** 很 重 要 。
Everyone thinks it is important to protect the **environment**.

307 会议   huì yì   **Noun:** meeting

秘_{mì} 书_{shū} 负_{fù} 责_{zé} 为_{wèi} 总_{zǒng} 裁_{cái} 安_{ān} 排_{pái} **会_{huì} 议_{yì}** 。

The secretary is responsible for arranging **meetings** for the president.

308 会员   huì yuán   **Noun:** membership; member

你_{nǐ} 也_{yě} 是_{shì} 自_{zì} 行_{xíng} 车_{chē} 俱_{jù} 乐_{lè} 部_{bù} 的_{de} **会_{huì} 员_{yuán}** 吗_{ma} ？

Are you also a **member** of the cycling club?

309 活   huó   **Verb:** to live; to be alive

他_{tā} **活_{huó}** 了_{le} 九_{jiǔ} 十_{shí} 岁_{suì} ， 去_{qù} 年_{nián} 死_{sǐ} 了_{le} 。

He **lived** to be ninety years old and died last year.

310 火   huǒ   **Noun:** fire; anger **Adjective:** popular

那_{nà} 栋_{dòng} 楼_{lóu} 着_{zháo} **火_{huǒ}** 了_{le} ， 快_{kuài} 去_{qù} 灭_{miè} **火_{huǒ}** ！

That building is on **fire**, go quickly to put out the **fire**!

你_{nǐ} 看_{kàn} 过_{guò} 他_{tā} 的_{de} 新_{xīn} 电_{diàn} 影_{yǐng} 吗_{ma} ？ 最_{zuì} 近_{jìn} 非_{fēi} 常_{cháng} **火_{huǒ}** ！

Have you seen his new movie? Very **popular** recently!

311 机器   jī qì   **Noun:** machine

这_{zhè} 些_{xiē} **机_{jī} 器_{qì}** 都_{dōu} 是_{shì} 德_{dé} 国_{guó} 生_{shēng} 产_{chǎn} 的_{de} 。

These **machines** are all made in Germany.

312 积极   jī jí   **Adjective:** enthusiastic

^{gōng}工 ^{chéng}程 ^{shī}师 ^{men}们 ^{dōu}都 ^{duì}对 ^{zhè}这 ^{gè}个 ^{xiàng}项 ^{mù}目 ^{hěn}很 ^{jī}**积** ^{jí}**极** 。

The engineers are all very **enthusiastic** about the project.

313 基本   jī běn   **Noun:** basis
                                                    Adjective: basic

Noun   ^{jī}积 ^{lěi}累 ^{cí}词 ^{huì}汇 ^{shì}是 ^{xué}学 ^{hǎo}好 ^{zhōng}中 ^{wén}文 ^{de}的 ^{jī}**基** ^{běn}**本** 。

Accumulating vocabulary is the **basis** for learning Chinese well.

Adj.   ^{wǒ}我 ^{men}们 ^{yào}要 ^{mǎn}满 ^{zú}足 ^{kè}客 ^{hù}户 ^{de}的 ^{jī}**基** ^{běn}**本** ^{yāo}要 ^{qiú}求 。

We need to satisfy the **basic** requirements of customers.

314 基本上   jī běn shàng   **Adverb:** basically

^{tā}他 ^{shì}是 ^{gè}个 ^{gōng}工 ^{zuò}作 ^{kuáng}狂 ，^{jī}**基** ^{běn}**本** ^{shàng}**上** ^{méi}没 ^{shí}时 ^{jiān}间 ^{xiū}休 ^{xi}息 。

He's a workaholic who **basically** has no time to rest.

315 基础   jī chǔ   **Noun:** foundation

^{chéng}诚 ^{xìn}信 ^{shì}是 ^{hé}合 ^{zuò}作 ^{de}的 ^{jī}**基** ^{chǔ}**础** 。

Honesty is the **foundation** of cooperation.

316 及时   jí shí   **Adverb:** in time

^{jǐng}警 ^{chá}察 ^{jí}**及** ^{shí}**时** ^{gǎn}赶 ^{dào}到 ^{le}了 ^{xiàn}现 ^{chǎng}场 。

The police arrived at the scene **in time**.

317 ...极了

... jí le

Adverb: extremely; exceedingly

nà chǎng shì gù kǒng bù **jí le**
那 场 事 故 恐 怖 **极 了** ！
The accident was **extremely** horrible!

318 集体

jí tǐ

Noun: collective; group

tīng shuō nà qún rén zài **jí tǐ** bà gōng
听 说 ， 那 群 人 在 **集 体** 罢 工 。
I heard that the group of people is on **collective** strike.

319 集中

jí zhōng

Verb: to focus

bié zǒng shì kàn shǒu jī yào **jí zhōng** zhù yì lì
别 总 是 看 手 机 ， 要 **集 中** 注 意 力 。
Don't always look at your phone, **focus** your attention.

320 计算

jì suàn

Verb: to calculate
Noun: calculation

Verb
tā **jì suàn** de fēi cháng zhǔn què
他 **计 算** 得 非 常 准 确 。
He **calculated** very accurately.

Noun
gēn jù tā de **jì suàn** chē chéng shì liǎng gè xiǎo shí
根 据 他 的 **计 算** ， 车 程 是 两 个 小 时 。
According to his **calculations**, the drive is two hours.

321 记录

jì lù

Verb: to record
Noun: record

Verb
jiān kòng qì **jì lù** le tā de zuì xíng
监 控 器 **记 录** 了 他 的 罪 行 。
Surveillance **recorded** his crime.

Noun
jiān kòng qì de **jì lù** jiù shì zhèng jù
监 控 器 的 **记 录** 就 是 证 据 。
The surveillance **records** are the evidence.

322 记者　　　jì zhě　　**Noun:** reporter

zhè gè kě lián de **jì zhě** bèi bǎo ān dǎ le
这 个 可 怜 的 **记 者** 被 保 安 打 了 。
The poor **reporter** was beaten by security guards.

323 纪录　　　jì lù　　**Noun:** record (achievement)

tā huò dé le guàn jūn dǎ pò le shì jiè **jì lù**
他 获 得 了 冠 军 ， 打 破 了 世 界 **纪 录** 。
He won the championship and broke the world **record**.

324 纪念　　　jì niàn　　**Verb:** in memory of; to commemorate　**Noun:** anniversary

Verb
duān wǔ jié shì wèi le **jì niàn** wěi dà shī rén qū yuán
端 午 节 是 为 了 **纪 念** 伟 大 诗 人 屈 原 。
The Dragon Boat Festival is to **commemorate** the great poet Qu Yuan.

Noun
míng tiān shì wǒ men jié hūn shí nián de **jì niàn** rì
明 天 是 我 们 结 婚 十 年 的 **纪 念** 日 。
Tomorrow is our ten year wedding **anniversary** (day).

325 技术　　　jì shù　　**Noun:** technology

gōng sī hěn kàn zhòng **jì shù** hé chuàng xīn
公 司 很 看 重 **技 术** 和 创 新 。
The company puts a lot of emphasis on **technology** and innovation.

326 继续　　　jì xù　　**Verb:** to continue

wǒ men yào **jì xù** gǎi shàn zhè gè ruǎn jiàn
我 们 要 **继 续** 改 善 这 个 软 件 。
We will **continue** to improve this software.

327 加工　jiā gōng　**Noun:** machining

qǐng wèn, **jiā gōng** fèi shì duō shǎo
请问，**加工**费是多少？
Excuse me, how much is the **machining** fee?

328 加快　jiā kuài　**Verb:** to speed up; to accelerate

kè hù yāo qiú **jiā kuài** chǎn pǐn de yùn shū
客户要求**加快**产品的运输。
The customer requested to **speed up** the shipping of the product.

329 加强　jiā qiáng　**Verb:** to strengthen; to reinforce

wǒ men yào **jiā qiáng** zhōng guó hé měi guó de hé zuò
我们要**加强**中国和美国的合作。
We need to **strengthen** cooperation between China and the United States.

330 家具　jiā jù　**Noun:** furniture

tā shì yì míng **jiā jù** shè jì shī
他是一名**家具**设计师。
He is a **furniture** designer.

331 家属　jiā shǔ　**Noun:** family (members)

jǐng chá lián xi le shòu hài zhě de **jiā shǔ**
警察联系了受害者的**家属**。
Police have contacted the victim's **family**.

332 家乡　jiā xiāng　**Noun:** hometown

wǒ de **jiā xiāng** yǒu yí gè měi lì de hú
我的**家乡**有一个美丽的湖。
My **hometown** has a beautiful lake.

333 价格　　jià gé　　**Noun:** price (formal)

<ruby>产<rt>chǎn</rt></ruby> <ruby>品<rt>pǐn</rt></ruby> <ruby>的<rt>de</rt></ruby> <ruby>价<rt>jià</rt></ruby> <ruby>格<rt>gé</rt></ruby> <ruby>可<rt>kě</rt></ruby> <ruby>以<rt>yǐ</rt></ruby> <ruby>协<rt>xié</rt></ruby> <ruby>商<rt>shāng</rt></ruby> <ruby>吗<rt>ma</rt></ruby> ？
Is the **price** of the product negotiable?

334 价钱　　jià qián　　**Noun:** price

<ruby>这<rt>zhè</rt></ruby> <ruby>件<rt>jiàn</rt></ruby> <ruby>西<rt>xī</rt></ruby> <ruby>装<rt>zhuāng</rt></ruby> <ruby>的<rt>de</rt></ruby> <ruby>价<rt>jià</rt></ruby> <ruby>钱<rt>qián</rt></ruby> <ruby>太<rt>tài</rt></ruby> <ruby>高<rt>gāo</rt></ruby> ， <ruby>我<rt>wǒ</rt></ruby> <ruby>买<rt>mǎi</rt></ruby> <ruby>不<rt>bu</rt></ruby> <ruby>起<rt>qǐ</rt></ruby> 。
The **price** of this suit is too high, I cannot afford it.

335 价值　　jià zhí　　**Noun:** value

<ruby>这<rt>zhè</rt></ruby> <ruby>部<rt>bù</rt></ruby> <ruby>电<rt>diàn</rt></ruby> <ruby>影<rt>yǐng</rt></ruby> <ruby>的<rt>de</rt></ruby> <ruby>艺<rt>yì</rt></ruby> <ruby>术<rt>shù</rt></ruby> <ruby>价<rt>jià</rt></ruby> <ruby>值<rt>zhí</rt></ruby> <ruby>很<rt>hěn</rt></ruby> <ruby>高<rt>gāo</rt></ruby> 。
The artistic **value** of this film is very high.

336 架　　jià　　**Noun:** frame; rack; shelf

<ruby>他<rt>tā</rt></ruby> <ruby>的<rt>de</rt></ruby> <ruby>书<rt>shū</rt></ruby> <ruby>架<rt>jià</rt></ruby> <ruby>上<rt>shàng</rt></ruby> <ruby>大<rt>dà</rt></ruby> <ruby>概<rt>gài</rt></ruby> <ruby>有<rt>yǒu</rt></ruby> <ruby>一<rt>yī</rt></ruby> <ruby>百<rt>bǎi</rt></ruby> <ruby>本<rt>běn</rt></ruby> <ruby>书<rt>shū</rt></ruby> 。
There are about a hundred books on his **shelf**.

337 坚持　　jiān chí　　**Verb:** to persist: to continue

<ruby>他<rt>tā</rt></ruby> <ruby>每<rt>měi</rt></ruby> <ruby>天<rt>tiān</rt></ruby> <ruby>晚<rt>wǎn</rt></ruby> <ruby>上<rt>shàng</rt></ruby> <ruby>都<rt>dōu</rt></ruby> <ruby>坚<rt>jiān</rt></ruby> <ruby>持<rt>chí</rt></ruby> <ruby>看<rt>kàn</rt></ruby> <ruby>书<rt>shū</rt></ruby> 。
He **continues** to read books every night.

338 坚决　　jiān jué　　**Adjective:** firm (attitude)

<ruby>他<rt>tā</rt></ruby> <ruby>的<rt>de</rt></ruby> <ruby>态<rt>tài</rt></ruby> <ruby>度<rt>dù</rt></ruby> <ruby>非<rt>fēi</rt></ruby> <ruby>常<rt>cháng</rt></ruby> <ruby>坚<rt>jiān</rt></ruby> <ruby>决<rt>jué</rt></ruby> 。
His attitude is very **firm**.

339 坚强　　　jiān qiáng　　**Adjective: strong (mentally)**

tā shì yí gè yòu jiān qiáng yòu lè guān de rén
他 是 一 个 又 **坚 强** 又 乐 观 的 人 。
He is a **strong** and positive person.

340 简单　　　jiǎn dān　　**Adjective: simple**

wǒ xǐ huān jiǎn dān de shēng huó fāng shì
我 喜 欢 **简 单** 的 生 活 方 式 。
I like the **simple** life style.

341 简直　　　jiǎn zhí　　**Adverb: simply**

gēn tā huán yóu shì jiè jiǎn zhí tài bàng le
跟 她 环 游 世 界 **简 直** 太 棒 了 ！
Traveling the world with her has been **simply** amazing!

342 建　　　jiàn　　**Verb: to build/ construct (physical)**

wǒ men xiǎng shēn qǐng zài zhè lǐ jiàn yí dòng fáng zi
我 们 想 申 请 在 这 里 **建** 一 栋 房 子 。
We want to apply **to build** a house here.

343 建成　　　jiàn chéng　　**Verb: to manage to build**

fáng zi jiàn chéng hòu wǒ men dǎ suàn zì jǐ zhù
房 子 **建 成** 后 ， 我 们 打 算 自 己 住 。
After we **manage to build** the house, we plan to live in it by ourselves.

344 建立　　　jiàn lì　　**Verb: to establish**

wǒ de mèng xiǎng shì jiàn lì zì jǐ de gōng sī
我 的 梦 想 是 **建 立** 自 己 的 公 司 。
My dream is **to establish** my own company.

345 建设 jiàn shè **Verb:** to build/ construct (abstract)

现在的首要任务是建设经济。
xiàn zài de shǒu yào rèn wù shì jiàn shè jīng jì

The priority task now is **to build** the economy.

346 建议 jiàn yì **Verb:** to propose; to suggest
Noun: proposal; suggestion

Verb
我建议他们找机会吸引外资。
wǒ jiàn yì tā men zhǎo jī huì xī yǐn wài zī

I **suggest** they look for opportunities to attract foreign investment.

Noun
他们对这个建议很感兴趣。
tā men duì zhè gè jiàn yì hěn gǎn xìng qù

They are very interested in this **proposal**.

347 将近 jiāng jìn **Adverb:** nearly

我的狗将近十二岁了，仍然很健康。
wǒ de gǒu jiāng jìn shí èr suì le， réng rán hěn jiàn kāng

My dog is **almost** twelve years old, and is still healthy.

348 将来 jiāng lái **Noun:** future

我要为我们的将来存钱。
wǒ yào wèi wǒ men de jiāng lái cún qián

I want to save money for our **future**.

349 交费 jiāo fèi **Verb:** to pay fee

请用银行转账交费。
qǐng yòng yín háng zhuǎn zhàng jiāo fèi

Please **pay the fee** by bank transfer.

350 交警   jiāo jǐng   **Noun:** traffic police

^{tā} ^{jiǔ} ^{jià}   ^{bèi} ^{jiāo} ^{jǐng} ^{fá} ^{le} ^{yī} ^{bǎi} ^{měi} ^{yuán}
他 酒 驾 ， 被 **交 警** 罚 了 一 百 美 元 。

He was fined a hundred dollars by the **traffic police** for drunk driving.

---

351 交流   jiāo liú   **Verb:** to exchange; to communicate
Noun: communication

Verb   ^{wǒ} ^{men} ^{jiāo} ^{liú} ^{le} ^{bù} ^{tóng} ^{de} ^{kuà} ^{wén} ^{huà} ^{jīng} ^{yàn}
我 们 **交 流** 了 不 同 的 跨 文 化 经 验 。

We **exchanged** different cross-cultural experiences.

Noun   ^{cù} ^{jìn} ^{kuà} ^{wén} ^{huà} ^{jiāo} ^{liú} ^{duì} ^{wǒ} ^{men} ^{hěn} ^{zhòng} ^{yào}
促 进 跨 文 化 **交 流** 对 我 们 很 重 要 。

Increasing intercultural **communication** is important to us.

---

352 交往   jiāo wǎng   **Verb:** to date (getting along)

^{tā} ^{men} ^{jiāo} ^{wǎng} ^{sān} ^{nián} ^{hòu} ^{jué} ^{dìng} ^{jié} ^{hūn}
他 们 **交 往** 三 年 后 决 定 结 婚 。

They decided to get married after **dating** for three years.

---

353 交易   jiāo yì   **Noun:** transaction; trade

^{xìng} ^{jiāo} ^{yì} ^{zài} ^{duō} ^{shù} ^{guó} ^{jiā} ^{shì} ^{wéi} ^{fǎ} ^{de}
性 **交 易** 在 多 数 国 家 是 违 法 的 。

Sex **trade** is illegal in most countries.

---

354 叫   jiào   **Verb:** to call; to shout

^{zhè} ^{shì} ^{wǒ} ^{de} ^{wèi} ^{hūn} ^{qī}   ^{jiào} ^{xiǎo} ^{yún}
这 是 我 的 未 婚 妻 ， **叫** 小 云 。

This is my fiancée, **called** Xiaoyun.

355 较   jiào   **Adverb:** relatively; comparatively

gēn yīng guó bǐ, dé guó de tiān qì jiào hǎo
跟 英 国 比 , 德 国 的 天 气 较 好 。
Compared with the UK, Germany's weather is **relatively** better.

356 教材   jiào cái   **Noun:** textbook; teaching material

zhè běn jiào cái fēi cháng shí yòng, wǒ tuī jiàn
这 本 **教 材** 非 常 实 用 , 我 推 荐 。
This **textbook** is very practical, I recommend it.

357 教练   jiào liàn   **Noun:** coach

tā shì xī bān yá zuì yǒu míng de jiàn shēn jiào liàn
他 是 西 班 牙 最 有 名 的 健 身 **教 练** 。
He is the most famous fitness **coach** in Spain.

358 结实   jiē shi   **Noun:** muscular; strong (physical)

tā jī ròu fā dá, shēn tǐ fēi cháng jié shi
他 肌 肉 发 达 , 身 体 非 常 **结 实** 。
He has well-developed muscles, and has a very **strong** body.

359 接待   jiē dài   **Verb:** to receive **Noun:** reception

Verb
zǒng jīng lǐ zài huì yì shì jiē dài kè hù
总 经 理 在 会 议 室 **接 待** 客 户 。
The CEO is **receiving** clients in the conference room.

Noun
tā men duì zhè cì jiē dài hěn mǎn yì
他 们 对 这 次 **接 待** 很 满 意 。
They are very satisfied with the **reception**.

360 接近   jiē jìn   **Verb:** to near; to approach

_{tā} _{de} _{zhōng} _{wén} _{jiē} _{jìn} _{zhōng} _{jí} _{shuǐ} _{píng}
他 的 中 文 **接 近** 中 级 水 平 。

His Chinese is **nearing** intermediate level.

361 节约   jié yuē   **Verb:** to save (opposite to waste)

_{yào} _{xiǎng} _{bàn} _{fǎ} _{jié} _{yuē} _{shí} _{jiān} _{ér} _{bú} _{shì} _{làng}
要 想 办 法 **节 约** 时 间 ， 而 不 是 浪
_{fèi} _{shí} _{jiān}
费 时 间 。

We need to find ways **to save** time, instead of wasting it.

362 结合   jié hé   **Noun:** combination; integrated

_{tā} _{zài} _{zhōng} _{xī} _{yī} _{jié} _{hé} _{yī} _{yuàn} _{shàng} _{bān}
她 在 中 西 医 **结 合** 医 院 上 班 。

She works at an **integrated** Chinese-Western medicine hospital.

363 结婚   jié hūn   **Verb:** to marry

_{tā} _{hé} _{xiǎo} _{jiāng} _{jié} _{hūn} _{liǎng} _{nián} _{bàn} _{le}
她 和 小 江 **结 婚** 两 年 半 了 。

She and Xiaojiang have been **married** for two and a half years.

364 结束   jié shù   **Verb:** to end

_{kě} _{xī} _{tā} _{men} _{de} _{hūn} _{yīn} _{gāng} _{gāng} _{jié} _{shù} _{le}
可 惜 ， 他 们 的 婚 姻 刚 刚 **结 束** 了 。

Unfortunately, their marriage just **ended**.

365 解决   jiě jué   **Verb:** to resolve; to settle

tā yào qǐng lǜ shī bāng tā jiě jué lí hūn sù sòng
她 要 请 律 师 帮 她 **解 决** 离 婚 诉 讼 。
She wants to hire a lawyer to help her **settle** the divorce proceedings.

366 解开   jiě kāi   **Verb:** to untie

hái méi tíng chē qǐng bú yào jiě kāi ān quán dài
还 没 停 车 ， 请 不 要 **解 开** 安 全 带 。
The car has not stopped yet, please don't **untie** your seat belt.

367 金   jīn   **Noun:** gold

wǒ de jiè zhǐ shì chún jīn de tā de shì chún
我 的 戒 指 是 纯 **金** 的 ， 她 的 是 纯
yín de
银 的 。
My ring is solid **gold** and hers is solid silver.

368 金牌   jīn pái   **Noun:** gold medal

tā zài ào yùn huì shàng ná dào le jīn pái
他 在 奥 运 会 上 拿 到 了 **金 牌** 。
He obtained the **gold medal** in the Olympics.

369 仅(仅)   jǐn jǐn   **Adverb:** merely; only

cóng běi jīng zuò gāo tiě dào shàng hǎi jǐn sì gè bàn
从 北 京 坐 高 铁 到 上 海 **仅** 四 个 半
xiǎo shí
小 时 。
It takes **only** four and a half hours from Beijing to Shanghai by high-speed train.

370 尽量   jǐn liàng   **Adverb:** try one's best (at something)

bié dān xīn ， wǒ men huì jǐn liàng bāng nǐ chóu qián
别 担 心 , 我 们 会 尽 量 帮 你 筹 钱 。

Don't worry, we'll **try** our **best** to raise money for you.

371 紧   jǐn   **Adjective:** tight; strict

zhè tiáo tuǐ wà chǐ cùn bù hé shì ， wǒ chuān zhe
这 条 腿 袜 尺 寸 不 合 适 , 我 穿 着

tài jǐn
太 紧 。

These leg socks are not the right size, they are too **tight** for me.

372 紧急   jǐn jí   **Adjective:** urgent

xiàn zài qíng kuàng jǐn jí ， kuài diǎn bào jǐng
现 在 情 况 紧 急 , 快 点 报 警 。

The situation is **urgent** now, please call the police quickly.

373 紧张   jǐn zhāng   **Adjective:** nervous

miàn shì de shí hòu ， wǒ fēi cháng jǐn zhāng
面 试 的 时 候 , 我 非 常 紧 张 。

During the interview, I was very **nervous**.

374 进步   jìn bù   **Verb:** to progress

lǎo shī shuō wǒ de zhōng wén jìn bù de hěn kuài
老 师 说 我 的 中 文 进 步 得 很 快 !

The teacher said that my Chinese is **improving** very fast!

375 进一步　　jìn yi bù　　**Adverb:** further; go a step further

wǒ men yào jìn yi bù jiā qiáng hé zuò guān xi
我 们 要 进 一 步 加 强 合 作 关 系 。
We need to **further** strengthen our partnership.

376 进展　　jìn zhǎn　　**Verb:** to progress

hé tóng jìn zhǎn de zěn me yàng le
合 同 进 展 得 怎 么 样 了 ？
How is the contract **progressing**?

377 近期　　jìn qī　　**Noun:** recent times; near future

wǒ hé wǒ lǎo gōng jìn qī bù dǎ suàn yào hái zi
我 和 我 老 公 近 期 不 打 算 要 孩 子 。
My husband and I do not plan to have children in the **near future**.

378 京剧　　jīng jù　　**Noun:** Beijing Opera

nǐ kàn guò jīng jù huò chuān jù ma
你 看 过 京 剧 或 川 剧 吗 ？
Have you ever watched **Beijing Opera** or Sichuan Opera?

379 经济　　jīng jì　　**Noun:** economy

jīng jì fā zhǎn duì měi gè guó jiā dōu hěn zhòng yào
经 济 发 展 对 每 个 国 家 都 很 重 要 。
Economic development is important to every country.

73

380 经历   jīng lì

Verb: to experience
Noun: experience (personal)

Verb
wǒ men yì qǐ jīng lì le hěn duō dà qǐ dà luò
我 们 一 起 经 历 了 很 多 大 起 大 落 。
We've **experienced** a lot of ups and downs together.

Noun
zhè xiē jīng lì ràng wǒ men gèng xìn rèn duì fāng
这 些 经 历 让 我 们 更 信 任 对 方 。
These **experiences** made us trust each other even more.

381 经验   jīng yàn

Noun: experience (professional)

tā zài yà zhōu hé ōu zhōu dōu yǒu fēng fù de gōng
他 在 亚 洲 和 欧 洲 都 有 丰 富 的 工
zuò jīng yàn
作 经 验 。
He has rich working **experience** in both Asia and Europe.

382 经营   jīng yíng

Verb: to operate; to manage (business)
Noun: management

Verb
tā bǎ wǎng diàn jīng yíng de hěn hǎo
她 把 网 店 经 营 得 很 好 ！
She **manages** the online shop very well!

Noun
wǒ hěn xǐ huān tā de jīng yíng fāng shì
我 很 喜 欢 她 的 经 营 方 式 。
I like her way of **management**.

383 精彩   jīng cǎi

Adjective: splendid; astonishing (for shows or movies)

zhè chǎng bā lěi wǔ biǎo yǎn zhēn shì tài jīng cǎi le
这 场 芭 蕾 舞 表 演 真 是 太 精 彩 了 ！
The ballet performance is truly so **splendid**!

384 精神   jīng shén   **Noun:** spirit; mind
                                              Adjective: lively; vigor

Noun
hái zi bìng le   jīng shén bú tài hǎo
孩 子 病 了 ， **精 神** 不 太 好 ！
The child is sick and not in good **spirits**!

Adj.
děng tā huī fù le   yí dìng huì hěn jīng shén
等 他 恢 复 了 ， 一 定 会 很 **精 神** 。
When he recovers, he will definitely be **lively**.

385 景色   jǐng sè   **Noun:** scenery

wǒ ài shàng le fǎ guó nán bù de hǎi àn jǐng sè
我 爱 上 了 法 国 南 部 的 海 岸 **景 色** 。
I've fallen in love with the coastal **scenery** in the south of France.

386 警察   jǐng chá   **Noun:** police

xiǎo tōu gāng gāng bèi jǐng chá dài bǔ le
小 偷 刚 刚 被 **警 察** 逮 捕 了 。
The thief has just been arrested by the **police**.

387 静   jìng   **Adjective:** silent; quiet

xiǎo qū wǎn shàng qī diǎn zuì chǎo shí yī diǎn zuì jìng
小 区 晚 上 七 点 最 吵 ， 十 一 点 最 **静** 。
The neighborhood is the noisiest at 7pm and the **quiet**est at 11pm.

388 久   jiǔ   **Adjective:** long (time)

wǒ hěn jiǔ méi yǒu hé tā qù jiǔ ba le
我 很 **久** 没 有 和 他 去 酒 吧 了 。
I haven't gone to the bar with him for a **long** time.

389 旧   jiù   **Adjective:** old; used

zhè jiàn jiù yī fu shì shí nián qián mǎi de
这 件 **旧** 衣 服 是 十 年 前 买 的 。
This **old** clothing was bought ten years ago.

390 救   jiù   **Verb:** to save (life or situation)

zāo gāo hái zi diào shuǐ le kuài qù jiù tā
糟 糕 ！ 孩 子 掉 水 了 ， 快 去 **救** 他 。
Oops! The child fell into the water, quickly go **save** him.

391 就是   jiù shì   **Adverb:** precisely; exactly; just

zhè gè míng xīng jiù shì tài shuài suǒ yǐ yǒu hěn
这 个 明 星 **就 是** 太 帅 ， 所 以 有 很
duō fěn sī
多 粉 丝 。
This star is **just** too handsome, so he has many fans.

392 就业   jiù yè   **Verb:** to take up an occupation

tā èr shí yī suì kāi shǐ jiù yè
他 二 十 一 岁 开 始 **就 业** 。
He started **taking up an occupation** at the age of 21.

393 举办   jǔ bàn   **Verb:** to host; to hold

wǒ zhǔn bèi zài jiā jǔ bàn shēng rì jù huì
我 准 备 在 家 **举 办** 生 日 聚 会 。
I'm going to **host** a birthday party at home.

394 具体   jù tǐ   **Adjective:** specific
Adverb: specifically

Adj.

bú yào cuò guò zhè xiē jù tǐ de xì jié
不 要 错 过 这 些 **具 体** 的 细 节 。
Don't miss these **specific** details.

Adv.

nǐ jù tǐ xiǎng yāo qǐng nǎ xiē péng yǒu
你 **具 体** 想 邀 请 哪 些 朋 友 ？
Which friends **specifically** do you want to invite?

395 具有   jù yǒu   **Verb:** to possess; to have

tā de gē shēng hěn měi jù yǒu yīn yuè tiān fù
她 的 歌 声 很 美 ， **具 有** 音 乐 天 赋 。
Her singing voice is beautiful, and **has** musical talent.

396 剧场   jù chǎng   **Noun:** theater

dǎo yǎn xiǎng yāo qǐng tā qù jù chǎng biǎo yǎn
导 演 想 邀 请 她 去 **剧 场** 表 演 。
The director wants to invite her to perform in the **theater**.

397 据说   jù shuō   **Conjunction:** it is said; allegedly

jù shuō zhè shì tā de dì yī cì wǔ tái biǎo yǎn
据 说 ， 这 是 她 的 第 一 次 舞 台 表 演 。
It is said that this is her first stage performance.

398 决定   jué dìng   **Verb:** to decide
Noun: decision

Verb

wǒ jué dìng xiàng tā qiú hūn
我 **决 定** 向 她 求 婚 。
I've **decided** to propose to her.

Noun

nǐ men cái jiāo wǎng sān gè yuè zhè gè jué dìng hé shì ma
你 们 才 交 往 三 个 月 ， 这 个 **决 定** 合 适 吗 ？
You have only been dating for three months, is this **decision** appropriate?

399 决赛

jué sài

Noun: final (competition)

shì jiè bēi de **jué sài** mǎ shàng jiù kāi shǐ le
世 界 杯 的 **决 赛** 马 上 就 开 始 了 。
The World Cup **final** is about to begin.

400 决心

jué xīn

Noun: determination

zhè gè qiú duì yǒu **jué xīn** yíng dé guàn jūn ma
这 个 球 队 有 **决 心** 赢 得 冠 军 吗 ？
Does this team have the **determination** to win a championship?

401 绝对

jué duì

Adjective: absolute

wǒ duì tā men yǒu **jué duì** de xìn xīn
我 对 他 们 有 **绝 对** 的 信 心 。
I have **absolute** confidence in them.

402 咖啡

kā fēi

Noun: coffee

zhè xiē **kā fēi** dōu shì cóng fēi zhōu jìn kǒu de
这 些 **咖 啡** 都 是 从 非 洲 进 口 的 。
These **coffees** are all imported from Africa.

403 开发

kāi fā

Verb: to develop (products or land)

jì shù bù mén zài **kāi fā** xīn de ruǎn jiàn
技 术 部 门 在 **开 发** 新 的 软 件 。
The technical department is **developing** new software.

404 开放　　kāi fàng

Verb: to open up
Adjective: open minded

Verb
gǔ piào shì chǎng shén me shí hòu kāi fàng
股 票 市 场 什 么 时 候 开 放？
When is the stock market **opening up**?

Adj.
nián qīng rén de sī xiǎng yuè lái yuè kāi fàng
年 轻 人 的 思 想 越 来 越 开 放。
Young people's minds are becoming more and more **open**.

405 开始　　kāi shǐ

Verb: to start

wǒ shì cóng qù nián kāi shǐ tóu zī fáng dì chǎn de
我 是 从 去 年 开 始 投 资 房 地 产 的。
I have **started** investing in real estate since last year.

406 开业　　kāi yè

Verb:
to open business

míng tiān gōng sī huì zhèng shì kāi yè huān yíng lái
明 天 公 司 会 正 式 开 业， 欢 迎 来
cān guān
参 观。
Tomorrow the company will officially **open the business**,
welcome to visit.

407 开展　　kāi zhǎn

Verb: to run;
to launch (activity)

wǒ men yě huì kāi zhǎn cù xiāo huó dòng
我 们 也 会 开 展 促 销 活 动。
We will also **launch** promotional activities.

408 看起来　　kàn qǐ lái

Adverb: look (like)

tā wèi shén me kàn qǐ lái hěn jǐn zhāng
他 为 什 么 看 起 来 很 紧 张？
Why does he **look** so nervous?

409 看上去

kàn shàng qù

Adverb: seem to; seemingly

tā kàn shàng qù shì dì yī cì cān jiā yǎn jiǎng bǐ sài
他 看 上 去 是 第 一 次 参 加 演 讲 比 赛 。

He **seemed to** be attending a speech competition for the first time.

410 考验

kǎo yàn

Verb: to test
Noun: test

Verb

wǒ dǎ suàn zài qíng rén jié kǎo yàn yí xià wǒ de
我 打 算 在 情 人 节 考 验 一 下 我 的
nán péng yǒu
男 朋 友 。

I'm going **to test** my boyfriend a bit for Valentine's Day.

Noun

tā kě néng huì duì nǐ de kǎo yàn bù shū fu
他 可 能 会 对 你 的 考 验 不 舒 服 。

He may be uncomfortable with your **test**.

411 科技

kē jì

Noun: science and technology

gōng sī jīn nián zhǔ yào zài kē jì fāng miàn tóu zī
公 司 今 年 主 要 在 科 技 方 面 投 资 。

The company is investing mainly in **technology** this year.

412 可靠

kě kào

Adjective: reliable

qí shí yǒu qíng bǐ ài qíng gèng kě kào
其 实 , 友 情 比 爱 情 更 可 靠 。

In fact, friendship is more **reliable** than romantic love.

413 可乐

kě lè

Noun: coke; cola

tiān tiān hē kě lè duì jiàn kāng bù hǎo
天 天 喝 可 乐 对 健 康 不 好 。

Drinking **cola** every day is bad for health.

414 克服   kè fú   **Verb:** to overcome

rén de yì shēng yào kè fú hěn duō kùn nán
人 的 一 生 要 克 服 很 多 困 难 。
A person has **to overcome** many difficulties in their life.

415 客观   kè guān   **Adjective:** objective

shì shí shì kè guān de ， yì jiàn shì zhǔ guān de
事 实 是 客 观 的 ， 意 见 是 主 观 的 。
Facts are **objective**, opinions are subjective.

416 课程   kè chéng   **Noun:** curriculum; course

wǒ zài wǎng shàng mǎi le yí tào jīn róng kè chéng
我 在 网 上 买 了 一 套 金 融 课 程 。
I bought a set of financial **courses** online.

417 空   kōng   **Adjective:** empty

wǒ de dù zi hěn kōng ， jué de fēi cháng è
我 的 肚 子 很 空 ， 觉 得 非 常 饿 。
My stomach is **empty** and I feel very hungry.

418 空调   kōng tiáo   **Noun:** air conditioner

gōng rén míng zǎo huì lái ān zhuāng kōng tiáo
工 人 明 早 会 来 安 装 空 调 。
Workers will come to install the **air conditioner** tomorrow morning.

419 恐怕   kǒng pà   be afraid that

wǒ kǒng pà míng tiān bù dé bù zài jiā shàng bān
我 恐 怕 明 天 不 得 不 在 家 上 班 。
I'm **afraid that** I'll have to work from home tomorrow.

420 空   kòng   **Noun:** free time

nǐ shén me shí hòu yǒu kòng gēn wǒ qù guàng jiē
你 什 么 时 候 有 **空** 跟 我 去 逛 街 ？
When do you have **free time** to go shopping with me?

421 裤子   kù zi   **Noun:** trousers

wǒ xiǎng qù mǎi yì tiáo kù zi hé yì shuāng xié zi
我 想 去 买 一 条 **裤 子** 和 一 双 鞋 子 。
I want to buy a pair of **trousers** and a pair of shoes.

422 快速   kuài sù   **Adjective:** quick; fast-speed

wǒ gāng gāng kàn dào yì zhī gē zi kuài sù de fēi guò
我 刚 刚 看 到 一 只 鸽 子 **快 速** 地 飞 过 。
I just saw a pigeon flying by at **fast-speed**.

423 困   kùn   **Adjective:** sleepy

wǒ zuó wǎn méi shuì hǎo suǒ yǐ jīn tiān hěn kùn
我 昨 晚 没 睡 好 ， 所 以 今 天 很 **困** 。
I didn't sleep well last night, so I'm very **sleepy** today.

424 困难   kùn nán   **Adjective:** difficult
                                     Noun: difficulty

Adj.
wǒ xiǎng shēng zhí dàn shì yǒu diǎn kùn nán
我 想 升 职 ， 但 是 有 点 **困 难** 。
I want to get promoted, but it's a bit **difficult**.

Noun
chéng gōng de lù shàng yǒu hěn duō kùn nán
成 功 的 路 上 有 很 多 **困 难** 。
There are many **difficulties** on the road to success.

425 浪费　　　làng fèi　　　**Verb: to waste**

wǒ gào sù hái zi bié suí biàn làng fèi qián
我 告 诉 孩 子 别 随 便 **浪 费** 钱 。
I tell my children not **to waste** money casually.

426 老百姓　　　lǎo bǎi xìng　　　**Noun: ordinary people**

zhàn zhēng yán zhòng yǐng xiǎng le lǎo bǎi xìng de shēng huó
战 争 严 重 影 响 了 **老 百 姓** 的 生 活 。
The war severely affected the lives of **ordinary people**.

427 老板　　　lǎo bǎn　　　**Noun: boss**

wǒ de lǎo bǎn shì yí gè yì wàn fù wēng
我 的 **老 板** 是 一 个 亿 万 富 翁 。
My **boss** is a billionaire.

428 老太太　　　lǎo tài tai　　　**Noun: old lady**

nà wèi lǎo tài tai jīn nián jiǔ shí bā suì le
那 位 **老 太 太** 今 年 九 十 八 岁 了 。
The **old lady** is ninety-eight years old this year.

429 老头　　　lǎo tóu　　　**Noun: old man**

páng biān de lǎo tóu shì tā de zhàng fu
旁 边 的 **老 头** 是 她 的 丈 夫 。
The **old man** next to her is her husband.

430 乐　　　lè　　　**Verb: to cheer**

gào sù wǒ nǐ zài lè shén me ne
告 诉 我 ， 你 在 **乐** 什 么 呢 ？
Tell me what are you **cheering** at?

431 乐观　　　lè guān　　　**Adjective:** optimistic; positive

她 以 前 有 点 悲 观 ， 但 是 现 在 很
tā yǐ qián yǒu diǎn bēi guān dàn shì xiàn zài hěn
乐 观 。
lè guān

She was a little pessimistic before, but now she is **optimistic**.

432 类　　　lèi　　　**Noun:** category; type; kind

我 的 书 架 上 有 不 同 类 的 书 。
wǒ de shū jià shàng yǒu bù tóng lèi de shū

There are different **kinds** of books on my bookshelf.

433 类似　　　lèi sì　　　**Verb:** similar to

我 喜 欢 类 似 旗 袍 的 中 国 衣 服 。
wǒ xǐ huān lèi shì qí páo de zhōng guó yī fú

I like the type of Chinese clothes that is **similar to** cheongsam.

434 离婚　　　lí hūn　　　**Verb:** to divorce

他 和 他 前 妻 离 婚 五 年 多 了 。
tā hé tā qián qī lí hūn wǔ nián duō le

He and his ex-wife have been **divorced** for more than five years.

435 里面　　　lǐ miàn　　　**Noun:** inside; interior

快 打 开 礼 物 ， 我 们 想 知 道 里 面
kuài dǎ kāi lǐ wù wǒ men xiǎng zhī dào lǐ miàn
是 什 么 ！
shì shén me

Quickly open the present, we want to know what's **inside**!

436 理发   lǐ fà   **Verb:** to cut hair (formal)

这 个 **理 发** 师 在 给 顾 客 **理 发** 。
zhè gè lǐ fà shī zài gěi gù kè lǐ fà

This barber (**hair cutting** master) is **cutting hair** for a customer.

437 理解   lǐ jiě   **Verb:** to understand
Noun: understanding

Verb 我 不 **理 解** 他 为 什 么 是 个 花 花 公 子 。
wǒ bù lǐ jiě tā wèi shén me shì gè huā huā gōng zǐ

I don't **understand** why he's a playboy.

Noun 他 不 在 乎 别 人 的 看 法 和 **理 解** 。
tā bú zài hu bié rén de kàn fǎ hé lǐ jiě

He doesn't care about other people's views or **understanding**.

438 理论   lǐ lùn   **Noun:** theory

这 些 **理 论** 知 识 有 点 难 懂 。
zhè xiē lǐ lùn zhī shi yǒu diǎn nán dǒng

These **theoretical** concepts are a bit difficult to comprehend.

439 理由   lǐ yóu   **Noun:** reason

我 有 一 百 个 **理 由** 甩 这 个 渣 男 ！
wǒ yǒu yī bǎi gè lǐ yóu shuǎi zhè gè zhā nán

I have a hundred **reasons** to dump this scumbag!

440 力   lì   **Noun:** force

这 里 的 风 **力** 太 强 ， 树 是 歪 的 。
zhè lǐ de fēng lì tài qiáng shù shì wāi de

The wind **force** here is so strong that the trees are crooked.

441 力量　lì liàng

Noun: strength; power (physical)

wǒ ér zi xiǎng dāng chāo rén， huò dé chāo lì liàng
我 儿 子 想 当 超 人 ， 获 得 超 **力 量** 。
My son wants to be superman and gain super **powers**.

442 立刻　lì kè

Adverb: immediately

tā hěn shēng qì， lì kè ràng wǒ men bì zuǐ
他 很 生 气 ， **立 刻** 让 我 们 闭 嘴 ！
He was very angry and told us to shut up **immediately**!

443 利用　lì yòng

Verb: to utilize; to take advantage of

kē xué jiā zài lì yòng fēng lì fā diàn
科 学 家 在 **利 用** 风 力 发 电 。
Scientists are **utilizing** wind power to generate electricity.

444 连　lián

Conjunction: even

dà jiā dōu shuō tā pí qi chà lián tā bà yě tóng yì
大 家 都 说 他 脾 气 差 ， **连** 他 爸 也 同 意 。
Everyone said he had a bad temper, **even** his father agreed.

445 连忙　lián máng

Adverb: hurriedly; quickly

tā lián máng dào qiàn， rán hòu zǒu le
他 **连 忙** 道 歉 ， 然 后 走 了 。
He **quickly** apologized and left.

446 连续　lián xù

Adverb: continuously

tā lián xù kāi le wǔ gè xiǎo shí de huì
他 **连 续** 开 了 五 个 小 时 的 会 。
He held meetings for five hours **continuously**.

447 连续剧   lián xù jù   **Noun:** TV series; soap opera

zhè bù lián xù jù zuì jìn fēi cháng huǒ
这 部 **连 续 剧** 最 近 非 常 火 。
This **TV series** has been very popular recently.

448 联合   lián hé   **Verb:** to unite
Noun: union; coalition

Verb
tā fù zé lián hé gè gè jī gòu yì qǐ yóu xíng
他 负 责 **联 合** 各 个 机 构 一 起 游 行 。
He is in charge of **uniting** various institutions together to protest.

Noun
zhèng fǔ xiǎng dǎ pò tā men de lián hé
政 府 想 打 破 他 们 的 **联 合** 。
The government wants to break their **union**.

449 联合国   lián hé guó   **Noun:** United Nations

tīng shuō lián hé guó de zǒng bù zài niǔ yuē
听 说 **联 合 国** 的 总 部 在 纽 约 。
I heard that the headquarters of the **United Nations** is in New York.

450 联系   lián xì   **Verb:** to contact
Noun: contact

Verb
wǒ hěn jiǔ méi yǒu hé qián nǚ yǒu lián xì le
我 很 久 没 有 和 前 女 友 **联 系** 了 。
I haven't **contacted** my ex-girlfriend for a long time.

Noun
wǒ men yǐ jīng duàn le lián xì
我 们 已 经 断 了 **联 系** 。
We have lost **contact**.

451 凉水   liáng shuǐ   **Noun:** cold water

tā shēng bìng de shí hòu bù xǐ huān hē liáng shuǐ
她 生 病 的 时 候 ， 不 喜 欢 喝 **凉 水** 。
When she is sick, she doesn't like to drink **cold water**.

452 了　le

Particle: indicate past tense; softens the tone

hěn kě xī， wǒ men yǐ jīng fēn shǒu le
很 可 惜 ， 我 们 已 经 分 手 了 。
Unfortunately, we have broken up.

bié kū le， tā bù zhí dé nǐ shāng xīn
别 哭 了 ， 他 不 值 得 你 伤 心 。
Don't cry, he doesn't deserve your sorrow.

453 领　lǐng

Verb: to lead; to receive

zhǔ guǎn fù zé lǐng wǒ men wán chéng xiàng mù
主 管 负 责 领 我 们 完 成 项 目 。
The director is responsible for **leading** us to complete the project.

nǐ duō shǎo suì kě yǐ lǐng yǎng lǎo jīn
你 多 少 岁 可 以 领 养 老 金 ？
At what age can you **receive** a pension?

454 领导　lǐng dǎo

Noun: leader

nǐ jué de wǒ men de zǒng tǒng shì gè hǎo lǐng dǎo ma
你 觉 得 我 们 的 总 统 是 个 好 领 导 吗 ？
Do you think our president is a good **leader**?

455 领先　lǐng xiān

Verb: to keep ahead

tā men de gōng sī zài fáng dì chǎn tóu zī fāng miàn
他 们 的 公 司 在 房 地 产 投 资 方 面
lǐng xiān
领 先 。
Their firm **keeps ahead** in the aspect of real estate investing.

456 另外   lìng wài

Conjunction: additionally

请 发 邮 件 通 知 大 家 ， **另 外** 请 订 会
qǐng fā yóu jiàn tōng zhī dà jiā   lìng wài qǐng dìng huì
议 室 。
yì shì

Please send an email to inform everyone, **additionally**, please book a conference room.

457 另一方面   lìng yì fāng miàn

Conjunction: on the other hand

一 方 面 他 说 爱 我 ， **另 一 方 面** 他 却
yì fāng miàn tā shuō ài wǒ   lìng yì fāng miàn tā què
和 别 人 约 会 。
hé bié rén yuē huì

On the one hand he says he loves me, **on the other hand** he's dating someone else.

458 留学   liú xué

Verb: to study overseas

我 朋 友 明 年 打 算 去 澳 洲 **留 学** 。
wǒ péng yǒu míng nián dǎ suàn qù ào zhōu liú xué

My friend plans to **study overseas** in Australia next year.

459 龙   lóng

Noun: dragon

我 老 婆 属 **龙** ， 比 我 大 一 岁 。
wǒ lǎo pó shǔ lóng bǐ wǒ dà yí suì

My wife is born in the year of **dragon**, and is one year older than me.

460 录   lù

Verb: to record (video or audio)

他 在 房 间 **录** 视 频 ， 不 要 打 扰 他 。
tā zài fáng jiān lù shì pín bú yào dǎ rǎo tā

He is **recording** videos in the room, don't disturb him.

461 录音   lù yīn   **Verb:** to do sound recording

wǒ xiǎng qǐng rén bāng wǒ lù yīn hé fān yì
我 想 请 人 帮 我 **录 音** 和 翻 译 。
I want to have someone **to do sound recording** and translation for me.

462 路线   lù xiàn   **Noun:** path; route

wǒ duì zhè tiáo lù xiàn bù shú xi nǐ kāi chē ba
我 对 这 条 **路 线** 不 熟 悉 , 你 开 车 吧 。
I'm not familiar with this **route**, please could you drive.

463 旅馆   lǚ guǎn   **Noun:** hostel

zhù bīn guǎn tài guì wǒ men zhù lǚ guǎn ba
住 宾 馆 太 贵 , 我 们 住 **旅 馆** 吧 。
It's too expensive to stay in a hotel, let's stay in a **hostel**.

464 旅行社   lǚ xíng shè   **Noun:** travel agency

zhè gè lǚ xíng shè de fú wù tài dù hěn hǎo
这 个 **旅 行 社** 的 服 务 态 度 很 好 。
The service attitude of this **travel agency** is very good.

465 绿茶   lǜ chá   **Noun:** green tea

wǒ zuì xǐ huān de zhōng guó lǜ chá shì bì luó chūn
我 最 喜 欢 的 中 国 **绿 茶** 是 碧 螺 春 。
My favorite Chinese **green tea** is Biluochun.

466 乱   luàn   **Adjective:** chaotic; messy

kè tīng tài luàn wǒ yào shōu shi yí xià
客 厅 太 **乱** , 我 要 收 拾 一 下 。
The living room is too **messy**, I need to tidy it up.

467 落后   luò hòu   **Verb:** to lag behind
Adjective: backward; underdeveloped

Verb
jiā yóu ! kuài diǎn pǎo , bú yào luò hòu !
加 油 ！ 快 点 跑 ， 不 要 落 后 ！
Come on! Run fast, don't **fall behind**!

Adj.
fēi zhōu yǒu yì xiē luò hòu de guó jiā 。
非 洲 有 一 些 落 后 的 国 家 。
There are some **underdeveloped** countries in Africa.

468 麻烦   má fan   **Adjective:** troublesome

zuò dàn gāo hěn má fan , dàn shì hěn zhí dé 。
做 蛋 糕 很 麻 烦 ， 但 是 很 值 得 。
Making cakes is **troublesome**, but it's worth it.

469 马   mǎ   **Noun:** horse

tā zuó tiān qí mǎ de shí hòu , shuāi dǎo le 。
他 昨 天 骑 马 的 时 候 ， 摔 倒 了 。
When he was riding a **horse** yesterday, he fell off.

470 满足   mǎn zú   **Verb:** to satisfy
Adjective: satisfied; content

Verb
wǒ men yào mǎn zú kè hù de xū qiú 。
我 们 要 满 足 客 户 的 需 求 。
We want to **satisfy** the needs of clients.

Adj.
tā men yòu gǎn jī yòu mǎn zú 。
他 们 又 感 激 又 满 足 。
They are grateful and **satisfied**.

471 慢慢   màn màn   **Adverb:** slowly

bié xiān jié hūn ， yào huā shí jiān màn màn liǎo jiě tā 。
别 先 结 婚 ， 要 花 时 间 慢 慢 了 解 他 。
Don't get married first, take the time to get to know him **slowly**.

472 毛   máo

Noun: fur (animal); a fractional unit of money in China;

wǒ de shā fā shàng yǒu hěn duō gǒu máo
我 的 沙 发 上 有 很 多 狗 **毛** 。
My sofa has lots of dog **hair** on.

dǎ zhé hòu zhè píng jiǔ cái jiǔ kuai jiǔ máo
打 折 后 ， 这 瓶 酒 才 九 块 九 **毛** 。
After the discount, this bottle of wine is only ￥9.90 (nine kaui and nine **mao**).

473 毛病   máo bìng

Noun: sickness (colloquial)

bié guǎn zhè gè qí pā tā yǒu máo bìng
别 管 这 个 奇 葩 ， 他 有 **毛 病** ！
Ignore this weirdo, he is sick (has **sickness**)!

474 没用   méi yòng

Adjective: useless

wǒ de jīng lǐ hěn méi yòng
我 的 经 理 很 **没 用** ！
My manager is very **useless**!

475 媒体   méi tǐ

Noun: media

nǐ xǐ huān yòng nǎ gè shè jiāo méi tǐ
你 喜 欢 用 哪 个 社 交 **媒 体** ？
Which social **media** do you like to use?

476 每   měi

Pronoun: each; every

wǒ měi zhōu liù dōu gěi fù mǔ dǎ diàn huà
我 **每** 周 六 都 给 父 母 打 电 话 。
I always call my parents **every** Saturday.

477 美   měi   **Adjective:** beautiful; pretty

tā de lán yǎn jīng yòu měi yòu mí rén
他 的 蓝 眼 睛 又 美 又 迷 人 ！
His blue eyes are **beautiful** and charming!

478 美好   měi hǎo   **Adjective:** fond; wonderful

zài xīn jiā pō de jià qī shì wǒ men měi hǎo de
在 新 加 坡 的 假 期 是 我 们 美 好 的
huí yì
回 忆 。
Our holiday in Singapore is a **fond** memory for us.

479 美丽   měi lì   **Adjective:** beautiful

wǒ men yì qǐ kàn le měi lì de rì chū
我 们 一 起 看 了 美 丽 的 日 出 。
We watched the **beautiful** sunrise together.

480 美食   měi shí   **Noun:** delicious food; delicacy; gourmet

wǒ hěn huái liàn táng rén jiē de měi shí
我 很 怀 恋 唐 人 街 的 美 食 。
I miss the **delicious food** in Chinatown.

481 美术   měi shù   **Noun:** fine art

wǒ de guī mì shì yì míng měi shù lǎo shī
我 的 闺 蜜 是 一 名 美 术 老 师 。
My best friend is a **fine art** teacher.

482 美元   měi yuán   **Noun:** U.S. dollar

zhè tiáo yín xiàng liàn sān shí wǔ měi yuán
这 条 银 项 链 三 十 五 **美 元** 。
This silver necklace is thirty-five **dollars**.

483 迷   mí   **Noun:** fan (follower)
Verb: to be lost

Noun
nà xiē qiú mí kàn shàng qù hěn fēng kuáng
那 些 球 **迷** 看 上 去 很 疯 狂 ！
Those football **fans** look crazy!

Verb
zāo gāo wǒ mí lù le shǒu jī yě méi xìn hào
糟 糕 ！ 我 **迷** 路 了 ， 手 机 也 没 信 号 。
Oops! I'm **lost** (road) and my phone has no signal.

484 米   mǐ   **Noun:** meter; rice

tā de shēn gāo shì yì mǐ bā wǔ
他 的 身 高 是 一 **米** 八 五 。
His height is 1.85 **meters**.

485 面对   miàn duì   **Verb:** to face

tā shì gè dǎn xiǎo guǐ bù gǎn miàn duì zì jǐ
他 是 个 胆 小 鬼 ， 不 敢 **面 对** 自 己
de cuò
的 错 ！
He is a coward who dares not **face** his own mistakes!

486 面积   miàn jī   **Noun:** size
(measure of area)

gōng yù de miàn jī shì jiǔ shí píng fāng mǐ
公 寓 的 **面 积** 是 九 十 平 方 米 。
The **size** of the apartment is ninety square meters.

487 民间   mín jiān   **Noun:** folk; among the people

_{wǒ} _{xǐ} _{huān} _{dú} _{zhōng} _{guó} _{de} _{mín} _{jiān} _{gù} _{shì}
我 喜 欢 读 中 国 的 **民 间** 故 事 。
I like reading Chinese **folk** tales.

488 民族   mín zú   **Noun:** ethnicity

_{zhōng} _{guó} _{yǒu} _{wǔ} _{shí} _{liù} _{gè} _{mín} _{zú}
中 国 有 五 十 六 个 **民 族** 。
China has fifty-six **ethnicities**.

489 明确   míng què   **Verb:** to make clear; to define
Adjective: clear

Verb
_{nǐ} _{yào} _{míng} _{què} _{zì} _{jǐ} _{de} _{rén} _{shēng} _{mù} _{biāo}
你 要 **明 确** 自 己 的 人 生 目 标 。
You need **to define** your purpose in life.

Adj.
_{tā} _{hái} _{méi} _{gěi} _{wǒ} _{yí} _{gè} _{míng} _{què} _{de} _{dá} _{fù}
他 还 没 给 我 一 个 **明 确** 的 答 复 。
He hasn't given me a **clear** answer yet.

490 明显   míng xiǎn   **Adjective:** obvious

_{hěn} _{míng} _{xiǎn} _{tā} _{shì} _{yí} _{gè} _{hěn} _{shí} _{máo} _{de} _{rén}
很 **明 显** ， 他 是 一 个 很 时 髦 的 人 。
It's **obvious** that he's a fashionable person.

491 命运   mìng yùn   **Noun:** fate

_{wǒ} _{cóng} _{lái} _{dōu} _{bù} _{xiāng} _{xìn} _{mìng} _{yùn} _{nǐ} _{ne}
我 从 来 都 不 相 信 **命 运** ， 你 呢 ？
I've never believed in **fate**, how about you?

492 某　　　　　　　　　　mǒu　　　　**Pronoun:** some (unnamed)

新 闻 上 说 某 公 司 因 为 漏 税 被 罚
xīn wén shàng shuō mǒu gōng sī yīn wèi lòu shuì bèi fá
款 了 。
kuǎn le

The news said that **some** company was fined for evading taxes.

493 母亲　　　　　　　　mǔ qīn　　　　**Noun:** mother

我 的 母 亲 是 个 很 固 执 的 人 。
wǒ de mǔ qīn shì gè hěn gù zhí de rén

My **mother** is a very stubborn person.

494 木头　　　　　　　　mù tou　　　　**Noun:** wood

他 在 市 场 上 卖 木 头 。
tā zài shì chǎng shàng mài mù tou

He is selling **wood** in the market.

495 目标　　　　　　　　mù biāo　　　　**Noun:** goal; target

我 的 目 标 是 说 流 利 的 中 文 。
wǒ de mù biāo shì shuō liú lì de zhōng wén

My **goal** is to speak Chinese fluently.

496 目前　　　　　　　　mù qián　　　　**Noun:** at present

他 们 目 前 不 打 算 让 公 司 上 市 。
tā men mù qián bù dǎ suàn ràng gōng sī shàng shì

At present they are not planning to take the company public.

497 奶茶   nǎi chá   **Noun:** milk tea; bubble tea

zài dōng tiān , wǒ xǐ huān hē nǎi chá hé rè qiǎo
在 冬 天 ， 我 喜 欢 喝 **奶 茶** 和 热 巧
kè lì
克 力 。

In winter, I like to drink **bubble tea** and hot chocolate.

498 男子   nán zǐ   **Noun:** man; male

zhào shì nán zǐ dà gài wǔ shí duō suì
肇 事 **男 子** 大 概 五 十 多 岁 。

The **man** who caused the accident was probably in his fifties.

499 南部   nán bù   **Noun:** south

zhè shì měi guó nán bù zuì dà de qiāng shā shì jiàn
这 是 美 国 **南 部** 最 大 的 枪 杀 事 件 。

It was the largest mass shooting in the **south** of the USA.

500 难道   nán dào   **Particle:** indicates a rhetorical question

tài kǒng bù le nán dào zhè bú shì cǎn jù ma
太 恐 怖 了 ！ **难 道** 这 不 是 惨 剧 吗 ？

So horrible! Isn't this a tragedy?

501 难度   nán dù   **Noun:** difficulty (level)

tīng shuō zhuā huò zhè gè fàn rén de nán dù dà
听 说 抓 获 这 个 犯 人 的 **难 度** 大 。

I heard that it is difficult (big **difficulty**) to capture this criminal.

502 内　　　　　　nèi　　　　　　**Noun:** within; inner

_{jǐng} _{chá} _{dǎ} _{suàn} _{zài} _{sān} _{tiān} _{nèi} _{wán} _{chéng} _{zhuā} _{huò} _{rèn} _{wù}
警 察 打 算 在 三 天 **内** 完 成 抓 获 任 务 。
The police intend to complete the capture task **within** three days.

503 内容　　　　　nèi róng　　　　**Noun:** content

_{nǐ} _{kàn} _{guò} _{nà} _{fēng} _{qíng} _{shū} _{de} _{nèi} _{róng} _{ma}
你 看 过 那 封 情 书 的 **内 容** 吗 ？
Have you read the **contents** of that love letter?

504 内心　　　　　nèi xīn　　　　　**Noun:** inner (heart)

_{nǐ} _{liǎo} _{jiě} _{tā} _{de} _{nèi} _{xīn} _{qíng} _{gǎn} _{ma}
你 了 解 他 的 **内 心** 情 感 吗 ？
Do you understand his **inner** feelings?

505 能不能　　　　néng bu néng　　can or not

_{hěn} _{bào} _{qiàn} _{nǐ} _{néng} _{bu} _{néng} _{bì} _{zuǐ}
很 抱 歉 ， 你 **能 不 能** 闭 嘴 ？
Excuse me, **can** you shut up **or not**?

506 能力　　　　　néng lì　　　　　**Noun:** ability

_{tā} _{de} _{néng} _{lì} _{yǒu} _{xiàn} _{bù} _{néng} _{bāng} _{wǒ} _{men}
他 的 **能 力** 有 限 ， 不 能 帮 我 们 。
His **ability** is limited and cannot help us.

507 年初　　　　　nián chū　　　　　**Noun:**
　　　　　　　　　　　　　　　　　　　beginning of the year

_{zhè} _{gè} _{xiàng} _{mù} _{děi} _{zài} _{nián} _{chū} _{qǐ} _{dòng}
这 个 项 目 得 在 **年 初** 启 动 。
This project needs to start at the **beginning of the year**.

508 年底   nián dǐ   **Noun:** end of the year

wǒ bà huì zài nián dǐ tuì xiū
我 爸 会 在 **年 底** 退 休 。
My dad will retire at the **end of the year**.

509 年代   nián dài   **Noun:** era

zài nà gè nián dài   dà jiā zài zhōu rì dōu qù
在 那 个 **年 代**， 大 家 在 周 日 都 去
jiào táng
教 堂 。
In that **era**, everyone went to church on Sunday.

510 年纪   nián jì   **Noun:** age

zhāng jiào shòu de nián jì hěn dà   dàn shì hěn yōu mò
张 教 授 的 **年 纪** 很 大 ， 但 是 很 幽 默 。
Professor Zhang is very old (**age** big), but very humorous.

511 念   niàn   **Noun:** to read out

tā cháng cháng gěi wǒ men niàn jīng diǎn xiào huà
他 常 常 给 我 们 **念** 经 典 笑 话 。
He often **reads** classic jokes **out** for us.

512 牛   niú   **Noun:** cattle; ox; cow

wǒ de péng yǒu gù zhí de xiàng yì tóu niú
我 的 朋 友 固 执 得 像 一 头 **牛** 。
My friend is as stubborn as an **ox**.

513 农村   nóng cūn   **Noun:** countryside

yǒu xiē chéng shì rén kàn bu qǐ nóng cūn rén
有 些 城 市 人 看 不 起 **农 村** 人 。
Some city people look down on **countryside** people.

514 农民   nóng mín   **Noun:** farmer

wǒ wài gōng shì gè lǎo nóng mín， tā yǒu yí gè
我 外 公 是 个 老 **农 民** ， 他 有 一 个
dà nóng chǎng
大 农 场 。
My grandfather is an old **farmer**, he has a big farm.

515 农业   nóng yè   **Noun:** agriculture

kē jì tí gāo le nóng yè shēng chǎn lì
科 技 提 高 了 **农 业** 生 产 力 。
Technology has increased the productivity of **agriculture**.

516 女子   nǚ zǐ   **Noun:** woman; female

wǒ wài gōng nián qīng de shí hòu ài guò yí gè bā
我 外 公 年 轻 的 时 候 爱 过 一 个 巴
xī nǚ zǐ
西 **女 子** 。
My grandpa loved a Brazilian **woman** when he was young.

517 暖和   nuǎn huo   **Adjective:** warm

chūn tiān dào le， tiān qì biàn de nuǎn huo
春 天 到 了 ， 天 气 变 得 **暖 和** 。
Spring has arrived and the weather is getting **warm**.

518 怕　　　　　　pà　　　　　**Verb:** to fear; to be afraid of

tā lǎo pó shì mǔ lǎo hǔ，　tā dāng rán pà tā
他 老 婆 是 母 老 虎， 他 当 然 **怕** 她 。
His wife is a tigress, of course he is **afraid of** her.

519 拍　　　　　　pāi　　　　　**Verb:** to pat

tā pāi le hái zi de tóu，　rán hòu zǒu le
他 **拍** 了 孩 子 的 头， 然 后 走 了 。
He **patted** the child on the head, then left.

520 排　　　　　　pái　　　　　**Verb:** to rehearse; to put in order
　　　　　　　　　　　　　　　　　　Noun: row

Verb
kāi shǐ dēng jī le，　wǒ men qù pái duì ba
开 始 登 机 了， 我 们 去 **排** 队 吧 。
The boarding has started, let's queue up (**put** group **in order**).

Noun
wǒ men de zuò wèi zài dì liù pái
我 们 的 座 位 在 第 六 **排** 。
Our seats are in the sixth **row**.

521 排名　　　　　pái míng　　　　**Noun:** ranking

wǒ gào sù nǚ ér bú yào zài hū kǎo shì pái míng
我 告 诉 女 儿 不 要 在 乎 考 试 **排 名** 。
I told my daughter not to care about test **rankings**.

522 牌子　　　　　pái zi　　　　　**Noun:** brand; trademark

nǐ de chē zi shì shén me pái zi
你 的 车 子 是 什 么 **牌 子** ?
What's the **brand** of your car?

523 派   pài   **Verb:** to send

gōng sī pài tā xià gè yuè qù xiāng gǎng chū chāi
公 司 **派** 他 下 个 月 去 香 港 出 差 。
The company is **sending** him to Hong Kong for a business trip next month.

524 判断   pàn duàn   **Verb:** to judge
                                     Noun: judgement

Verb
wǒ men yào gēn jù shì shí pàn duàn qíng kuàng
我 们 要 根 据 事 实 **判 断** 情 况 。
We have **to judge** the situation based on the facts.

Noun
kě xī tā men de pàn duàn bú gòu zhǔn què
可 惜 ， 他 们 的 **判 断** 不 够 准 确 。
Unfortunately, their **judgments** were not accurate enough.

525 胖   pàng   **Adjective:** fat

tā bù xiǎng biàn pàng zuì jìn zài jiǎn féi
他 不 想 变 **胖** ， 最 近 在 减 肥 。
He doesn't want to get **fat** and is trying to lose weight recently.

526 跑步   pǎo bù   **Verb:** to run

wǒ měi tiān zǎo shàng pǎo bù bàn gè xiǎo shí
我 每 天 早 上 **跑 步** 半 个 小 时 。
I **run** for half an hour every morning.

527 配   pèi   **Verb:** to match;
                                     to mix (to a fixed ratio)

yī shēng de zhù lǐ zài gěi bìng rén pèi yào
医 生 的 助 理 在 给 病 人 **配 药** 。
The doctor's assistant is **mixing** the medicine for the patient.

528 配合　pèi hé　**Verb:** to cooperate (tasks)
Noun: cooperation

Verb
zài biǎo yǎn shàng, tā men **pèi hé** de hěn hǎo
在 表 演 上 ， 他 们 **配 合** 得 很 好 。
In the performance, they **cooperated** very well.

Noun
xiè xie nǐ de **pèi hé**, wǒ hěn gǎn jī
谢 谢 你 的 **配 合** ， 我 很 感 激 。
Thank you for your **cooperation**, I appreciate it.

529 批评　pī píng　**Verb:** to criticize
Noun: criticism

Verb
tā gāng gāng bèi tā de xiàn shàng jīng lǐ **pī píng** le
他 刚 刚 被 他 的 线 上 经 理 **批 评** 了 。
He's just been **criticized** by his line manager.

Noun
tā de xīn qíng bèi **pī píng** yǐng xiǎng le
他 的 心 情 被 **批 评** 影 响 了 。
His mood was affected by the **criticism**.

530 批准　pī zhǔn　**Verb:** to approve

tīng shuō, cǎi gòu fāng àn méi yǒu bèi **pī zhǔn**
听 说 ， 采 购 方 案 没 有 被 **批 准** 。
I heard that the procurement plan was not **approved**.

531 皮　pí　**Noun:** skin; leather

wǒ men jiā cóng lái bù mǎi **pí** shā fā
我 们 家 从 来 不 买 **皮** 沙 发 。
Our family never buys **leather** sofas.

532 皮包　pí bāo　**Noun:** purse; briefcase; leather bag

zhè gè **pí bāo** yuán jià 199 yuán, xiàn jià cái 88 yuán
这 个 **皮 包** 原 价 199 元 ， 现 价 才 88 元 。
The original price of this **leather bag** is 199 yuan, and the current price is only 88 yuan.

533 啤酒   pí jiǔ   **Noun:** beer

nǐ cān jiā guò dé guó de pí jiǔ jié ma
你 参 加 过 德 国 的 **啤 酒** 节 吗 ？
Have you ever attended Germany's **Beer** Festival?

534 票价   piào jià   **Noun:** fare; ticket price

cóng niǔ yuē dào bā lí de shāng wù cāng piào jià gāo ma
从 纽 约 到 巴 黎 的 商 务 舱 **票 价** 高 吗 ？
Is the business class **fare** from New York to Paris expensive?

535 评价   píng jià   **Verb:** to evaluate; to judge
Noun: evaluation

Verb
lǎo shī men zài píng jià cān sài zhě de biǎo xiàn
老 师 们 在 **评 价** 参 赛 者 的 表 现 。
The teachers are **evaluating** the performance of the contestants.

Noun
nǐ jué de tā men de píng jià gōng píng ma
你 觉 得 他 们 的 **评 价** 公 平 吗 ？
Do you think their **evaluation** is fair?

536 苹果   píng guǒ   **Noun:** apple

zài píng ān yè zhōng guó rén xǐ huān sòng píng guǒ
在 平 安 夜 ， 中 国 人 喜 欢 送 **苹 果** 。
On Christmas Eve, Chinese people like to gift **apples**.

537 破   pò   **Adjective:** torn; broken

zāo gāo wǒ de wà zi yòu pò le
糟 糕 ， 我 的 袜 子 又 **破** 了 。
Oops, my socks are **torn** again.

538 破坏   pò huài   **Verb:** to destroy

rèn hé shì dōu bù néng pò huài wǒ men de guān xi
任 何 事 都 不 能 **破 坏** 我 们 的 关 系 。

Nothing can **destroy** our relationship.

539 普遍   pǔ biàn   **Adjective:** universal; common

diàn nǎo hé píng bǎn zài xué xiào hěn pǔ biàn
电 脑 和 平 板 在 学 校 很 **普 遍** 。

Computers and tablets are **common** in schools.

540 普及   pǔ jí   **Verb:** to be spread widely

zhè zhǒng zhì liáo fāng fǎ hái méi yǒu pǔ jí yà zhōu
这 种 治 疗 方 法 还 没 有 **普 及** 亚 洲 。

This type of treatment has not yet **spread widely** in Asia.

541 期   qī   **Noun:** period; term

zǒng tǒng de rèn qī sì nián hòu huì jié shù
总 统 的 任 **期** 四 年 后 会 结 束 。

The president's **term** will end in four years.

542 齐   qí   **Verb:** to be level with
                                                Adjective: neat; even

Verb

tā de tóu fa qí jiān hěn piào liang
她 的 头 发 **齐** 肩 ， 很 漂 亮 。

Her hair **is level with** her shoulders and is beautiful.

Adj.

tā de liú hǎi hěn qí yǎn jīng dà dà de
她 的 刘 海 很 **齐** ， 眼 睛 大 大 的 。

Her bangs are **neat** and her eyes are big.

543 其次   qí cì   **Noun:** secondly

shǒu xiān tā shì zì yóu zhí yè zhě   qí cì tā dān shēn
首 先 她 是 自 由 职 业 者 ， **其 次** 她 单 身 。
Firstly she's a freelancer, **secondly** she's single.

544 其实   qí shí   **Adverb:** actually

tā de bèi jǐng qí shí hěn shén mì
她 的 背 景 **其 实** 很 神 秘 。
Her background is **actually** very mysterious

545 奇怪   qí guài   **Adjective:** odd; strange

tā hěn nián qīng xìng gé yǒu diǎn qí guài
她 很 年 轻 ， 性 格 有 点 **奇 怪** 。
She is very young and her personality is a bit **odd**.

546 气候   qì hòu   **Noun:** climate

běi fāng de qì hòu bú tài wěn dìng
北 方 的 **气 候** 不 太 稳 定 。
The **climate** in the north is not that stable.

547 千万   qiān wàn   **Adverb:** must

rú guǒ yǒu bào fēng xuě qiān wàn bié chū mén
如 果 有 暴 风 雪 ， **千 万** 别 出 门 。
If there's a snowstorm, you **must** not go out.

548 前后　　　qián hòu　　**Noun:** front and back; around

我 的 岳 父 岳 母 会 在 春 节 前 后 来
wǒ de yuè fù yuè mǔ huì zài chūn jié qián hòu lái
英 国 。
yīng guó

My parents-in-law will come to the UK **around** Chinese New Year.

549 前进　　　qián jìn　　**Verb:** to advance; to go forward

不 管 发 生 什 么 ， 我 都 会 前 进 ， 不
bù guǎn fā shēng shén me wǒ dōu huì qián jìn bú
会 后 退 。
huì hòu tuì

No matter what happens, I will **go forward**, not backward.

550 前面　　　qián miàn　　**Noun:** front

宾 馆 的 前 面 是 一 个 湖 ， 后 面 是 一
bīn guǎn de qián miàn shì yí gè hú hòu miàn shì yí
座 山 。
zuò shān

At the **front** of the hotel is a lake, at the back is a mountain.

551 前往　　　qián wǎng　　**Verb:** to go to; to leave for

我 的 团 队 明 天 会 坐 飞 机 前 往 广 州 。
wǒ de tuán duì míng tiān huì zuò fēi jī qián wǎng guǎng zhōu

My team will take an airplane **to go to** Guangzhou tomorrow.

552 强　　　qiáng　　**Adjective:** strong

他 以 前 很 弱 ， 现 在 很 强 。
tā yǐ qián hěn ruò xiàn zài hěn qiáng

He used to be weak, but now he is **strong**.

553 强大　　qiáng dà　　**Adjective:** powerful; formidable

zài ōu zhōu　nǎ gè guó jiā zuì qiáng dà
在 欧 洲 ， 哪 个 国 家 最 **强 大** ？
In Europe, which country is the most **powerful**?

554 强调　　qiáng diào　　**Verb:** to emphasize

tā yì zhí zài qiáng diào bú yào làng fèi shí jiān
他 一 直 在 **强 调** 不 要 浪 费 时 间 。
He kept **emphasizing** not to waste time.

555 强烈　　qiáng liè　　**Adjective:** intense

ōu zhōu bēi de bǐ sài fēi cháng qiáng liè
欧 洲 杯 的 比 赛 非 常 **强 烈** 。
The competition in the European Cup is very **intense**.

556 桥　　qiáo　　**Noun:** bridge

xiān guò qiáo rán hòu yòu zhuǎn jiù dào le
先 过 **桥** ， 然 后 右 转 ， 就 到 了 。
Cross the **bridge** first, then turn right and you're there.

557 巧　　qiǎo　　**Adjective:** skillful; coincidental

wǒ men dōu xǐ huān chī huǒ guō zhēn qiǎo
我 们 都 喜 欢 吃 火 锅 ， 真 **巧** ！
We both love hot pot, truly **coincidental**!

558 亲　　　　　qīn

Verb: to kiss
Adjective: close; intimate

Verb
wǒ kě yǐ qīn nǐ de liǎn ma
我 可 以 亲 你 的 脸 吗 ？
May I **kiss** your cheek?

Adj.
wǒ hé jì mǔ de guān xi bù qīn
我 和 继 母 的 关 系 不 亲 。
My relationship with my stepmother is not **close.**

559 亲切　　　　qīn qiè

Adjective: kind; cordial

tā jiào wǒ de xiǎo míng ràng wǒ jué de hěn qīn qiè
他 叫 我 的 小 名 ， 让 我 觉 得 很 亲 切 。
He called me by my nickname, which made me feel very **cordial.**

560 亲人　　　　qīn rén

Noun: relative; family member

wǒ de gǒu yě shì wǒ de qīn rén
我 的 狗 也 是 我 的 亲 人 。
My dog is also my **family member.**

561 亲自　　　　qīn zì

Adverb: personally; in person

wǒ huì qīn zì qù fēi jī chǎng jiē fù mǔ
我 会 亲 自 去 飞 机 场 接 父 母 。
I will **personally** go to the airport to pick up my parents.

562 情感　　　　qíng gǎn

Noun: feeling; emotion

chéng rén de qíng gǎn shì jiè hěn fù zá
成 人 的 情 感 世 界 很 复 杂 。
The world of adult **emotions** is very complicated.

563 情况 qíng kuàng Noun: situation

wǒ bù liǎo jiě tā men de hūn yīn qíng kuàng
我 不 了 解 他 们 的 婚 姻 情 况 。
I don't know their marital **situation**.

564 请教 qǐng jiào Verb: to consult

wǒ kě yǐ qǐng jiào nǐ zěn me yòng zhè gè chéng xù ma
我 可 以 请 教 你 怎 么 用 这 个 程 序 吗 ？
May I **consult** you how to use this program?

565 庆祝 qìng zhù Verb: to celebrate

tā shēng zhí le hěn zhí dé qìng zhù
他 升 职 了 ， 很 值 得 庆 祝 ！
He is promoted, well worth **celebrating**!

566 球迷 qiú mí Noun: football fan

tīng shuō liǎng biān de qiú mí men zài dǎ jià
听 说 ， 两 边 的 球 迷 们 在 打 架 。
I heard that the **fans** on both sides are fighting.

567 区 qū Noun: area; district; region

chéng shì de dōng bù shì qióng rén qū xī bù shì
城 市 的 东 部 是 穷 人 区 ， 西 部 是
fù rén qū
富 人 区 。
The east of the city is the poor **area**, and the west is the rich **area**.

568 区别   qū bié   **Noun:** difference

qióng rén hé fù rén de shēng huó yǒu hěn dà de qū bié
穷 人 和 富 人 的 生 活 有 很 大 的 **区 别** 。
There is a big **difference** between the lives of the poor and the rich.

569 取消   qǔ xiāo   **Verb:** to cancel

wǒ de háng bān gāng gāng bèi qǔ xiāo le
我 的 航 班 刚 刚 被 **取 消** 了 ！
My flight was just **canceled**!

570 去世   qù shì   **Verb:** to pass away; to die

nǚ wáng qù shì le hěn duō rén cān jiā le zhuī dào huì
女 王 **去 世** 了 ， 很 多 人 参 加 了 追 悼 会 。
The Queen **passed away**, and many people attended the memorial service.

571 全场   quán chǎng   **Noun:** the whole audience

zài zàng lǐ shàng quán chǎng dōu hěn bēi shāng
在 葬 礼 上 ， **全 场** 都 很 悲 伤 。
At the funeral, the **whole audience** was sad.

572 全面   quán miàn   **Adverb:** thoroughly; comprehensively; completely

dāng shí gǔ shì quán miàn bēn kuì
当 时 ， 股 市 **全 面** 奔 溃 。
At that time, the stock market **completely** collapsed.

573 全球   quán qiú   **Noun:** global; whole world

rán hòu　quán qiú jīn róng wēi jī bào fā le
然 后 ， 全 球 金 融 危 机 爆 发 了 。
Then, the **global** financial crisis broke out.

574 缺 (少)   quē (shǎo)   **Verb:** to be short of; to lack

wǒ men bù mén bù quē shǎo xíng zhèng rén yuán
我 们 部 门 不 缺 少 行 政 人 员 。
Our department doesn't **lack** administrative staff.

575 缺点   quē diǎn   **Noun:** shortcoming; demerit

měi gè rén dōu yǒu yōu diǎn hé quē diǎn
每 个 人 都 有 优 点 和 缺 点 。
Everyone has merits and **demerits**.

576 确保   què bǎo   **Verb:** to ensure

yóu yǒng de shí hòu　yí dìng yào què bǎo ān quán
游 泳 的 时 候 ， 一 定 要 确 保 安 全 。
When swimming, you must **ensure** safety.

577 确定   què dìng   **Adjective:** be sure

nǐ què dìng yào cí zhí ma
你 确 定 要 辞 职 吗 ？
Are you **sure** you want to resign?

578 确实 què shí

Adverb: indeed; exactly

<ruby>我<rt>wǒ</rt></ruby> <ruby>给<rt>gěi</rt></ruby> <ruby>你<rt>nǐ</rt></ruby> <ruby>涨<rt>zhǎng</rt></ruby> <ruby>工<rt>gōng</rt></ruby> <ruby>资<rt>zī</rt></ruby> <ruby>吧<rt>ba</rt></ruby>， <ruby>公<rt>gōng</rt></ruby> <ruby>司<rt>sī</rt></ruby> <ruby>确<rt>què</rt></ruby> <ruby>实<rt>shí</rt></ruby> <ruby>离<rt>lí</rt></ruby> <ruby>不<rt>bu</rt></ruby> <ruby>开<rt>kāi</rt></ruby> <ruby>你<rt>nǐ</rt></ruby> 。

Let me increase your salary, the company **indeed** cannot do without you.

579 裙子 qún zi

Noun: skirt; dress

<ruby>我<rt>wǒ</rt></ruby> <ruby>和<rt>hé</rt></ruby> <ruby>她<rt>tā</rt></ruby> <ruby>买<rt>mǎi</rt></ruby> <ruby>了<rt>le</rt></ruby> <ruby>一<rt>yí</rt></ruby> <ruby>样<rt>yàng</rt></ruby> <ruby>的<rt>de</rt></ruby> <ruby>裙<rt>qún</rt></ruby> <ruby>子<rt>zi</rt></ruby> 。

I bought the same **dress** as her.

580 群 qún

Noun: group

<ruby>大<rt>dà</rt></ruby> <ruby>家<rt>jiā</rt></ruby> <ruby>在<rt>zài</rt></ruby> <ruby>微<rt>wēi</rt></ruby> <ruby>信<rt>xìn</rt></ruby> <ruby>群<rt>qún</rt></ruby> <ruby>给<rt>gěi</rt></ruby> <ruby>她<rt>tā</rt></ruby> <ruby>送<rt>sòng</rt></ruby> <ruby>祝<rt>zhù</rt></ruby> <ruby>福<rt>fú</rt></ruby> 。

Everyone sent blessings to her in the WeChat **group**.

581 热爱 rè ài

Verb: to love ardently

<ruby>善<rt>shàn</rt></ruby> <ruby>良<rt>liáng</rt></ruby> <ruby>的<rt>de</rt></ruby> <ruby>人<rt>rén</rt></ruby> <ruby>都<rt>dōu</rt></ruby> <ruby>热<rt>rè</rt></ruby> <ruby>爱<rt>ài</rt></ruby> <ruby>和<rt>hé</rt></ruby> <ruby>平<rt>píng</rt></ruby> 。

Kind-hearted people all **love** peace **ardently**.

582 热烈 rè liè

Adjective: warm; cheerful (atmosphere)

<ruby>主<rt>zhǔ</rt></ruby> <ruby>持<rt>chí</rt></ruby> <ruby>人<rt>rén</rt></ruby> <ruby>给<rt>gěi</rt></ruby> <ruby>了<rt>le</rt></ruby> <ruby>嘉<rt>jiā</rt></ruby> <ruby>宾<rt>bīn</rt></ruby> <ruby>热<rt>rè</rt></ruby> <ruby>烈<rt>liè</rt></ruby> <ruby>的<rt>de</rt></ruby> <ruby>欢<rt>huān</rt></ruby> <ruby>迎<rt>yíng</rt></ruby> 。

The host gave the guests a **warm** welcome.

583 人才　rén cái

Noun: talented person

xīn wén jī gòu hěn quē zhè zhǒng rén cái
新 闻 机 构 很 缺 这 种 人 才 。
News organizations are in short supply of such **talented people**.

584 人工　rén gōng

Noun: artificial; manual work

rén gōng zhì néng fā zhǎn de hěn kuài
人 工 智 能 发 展 得 很 快 。
Artificial intelligence is developing rapidly.

585 人类　rén lèi

Noun: mankind

shèng jīng lǐ yǒu rén lèi qǐ yuán de gù shì
圣 经 里 有 人 类 起 源 的 故 事 。
There are stories of the origin of **mankind** in the Bible.

586 人民　rén mín

Noun: people (political term)

zhèng fǔ yīng gāi wèi rén mín fú wù
政 府 应 该 为 人 民 服 务 。
The government should serve the **people**.

587 人民币　rén mín bì

Noun: RMB (currency)

nín hǎo wǒ xiǎng yòng měi yuán duì huàn rén mín bì
您 好 ！ 我 想 用 美 元 兑 换 人 民 币 。
Hello! I want to exchange US dollars for **RMB**.

588 人群　rén qún

Noun: crowd

shì zhōng xīn dào chù dōu shì rén qún
市 中 心 到 处 都 是 人 群 。
The city center is full of **crowds** everywhere.

589 人生   rén shēng   **Noun:** life (formal)

wǒ de rén shēng yīn wèi wǒ de ài rén wán zhěng
我 的 **人 生** 因 为 我 的 爱 人 完 整 。
My **life** is complete because of my spouse.

590 人员   rén yuán   **Noun:** personnel; staff

rú guǒ yǒu wèn tí qǐng lián xì gōng zuò rén yuán
如 果 有 问 题 ， 请 联 系 工 作 **人 员** 。
If you have questions, please contact the (working) **staff**.

591 认出   rèn chū   **Verb:** to identify

jǐng chá tōng guò jiān kòng qì rèn chū le tā
警 察 通 过 监 控 器 **认 出** 了 他 。
Police **identified** him through surveillance cameras.

592 认得   rèn dé   **Verb:** to recognize

shòu hài zhě men yě shuō rèn dé tā
受 害 者 们 也 说 **认 得** 他 。
Victims also said they **recognized** him.

593 认可   rèn kě   **Verb:** to approve; to recognize
Noun: approval; recognition

Verb

lǎo shī hé tóng xué men dōu rèn kě wǒ de yǎn jiǎng
老 师 和 同 学 们 都 **认 可** 我 的 演 讲 。
Teachers and classmates all **approved** my speech.

Noun

wǒ hěn róng xìng néng dé dào tā men de rèn kě
我 很 荣 幸 能 得 到 他 们 的 **认 可** 。
I am honored to have gained their **recognition**.

594 任   rèn   **Verb:** to appoint; to assign
Conjunction: no matter

Verb

tā méi yǒu bèi **rèn** wéi fù zǒng tǒng
他 没 有 被 **任** 为 副 总 统 。
He is not **appointed** as vice president.

Conj.

rèn tā shēng qì ， wǒ yě yào gào sù tā zhēn xiàng
任 他 生 气 ， 我 也 要 告 诉 他 真 相 。
No matter how angry he is, I will tell him the truth.

595 任何   rèn hé   **Pronoun:** any; whatever

tā bèi chǎo le dàn shì méi yǒu gào sù **rèn hé** rén
他 被 炒 了 ， 但 是 没 有 告 诉 **任 何** 人 。
He was fired, but he didn't tell **any**one.

596 任务   rèn wu   **Noun:** task

tā zuì jìn **rèn wu** tài duō ， cháng cháng jiā bān
他 最 近 **任 务** 太 多 ， 常 常 加 班 。
He has too many **tasks** recently and often works overtime.

597 仍(然)   réng rán   **Adverb:** still; yet; remain

zhǐ shì ， lǎo bǎn **réng rán** méi yǒu gěi tā jiā bān fèi
只 是 ， 老 板 **仍 然** 没 有 给 他 加 班 费 。
However, the boss **still** doesn't give him overtime pay.

598 日常   rì cháng   **Adjective:** daily

wǒ men de **rì cháng** shēng huó lí bu kāi shǒu jī
我 们 的 **日 常** 生 活 离 不 开 手 机 。
Our **daily** life is inseparable from mobile phones.

599 容易   róng yì   **Adjective: easy**

tā shuō zuò píng guǒ bǐng hěn róng yì dàn wǒ jué
他 说 做 苹 果 饼 很 **容 易** ， 但 我 觉
de nán
得 难 。

He said it was **easy** to make apple pie, but I find it difficult.

600 如何   rú hé   how

rú hé àn zhào shí pǔ zuò shì chéng gōng de guān jiàn
如 何 按 照 食 谱 做 是 成 功 的 关 键 。

How to follow the recipe (to make) is the key to success.

601 散步   sàn bù   **Verb: to take a walk**

wǒ men xià wǔ qù gōng yuán sàn bù zěn me yàng
我 们 下 午 去 公 园 **散 步** ， 怎 么 样 ？

How about we **take a walk** in the park in the afternoon?

602 沙发   shā fā   **Noun: sofa**

wǒ shàng gè zhōu mǎi le yí tào èr shǒu shā fā
我 上 个 周 买 了 一 套 二 手 **沙 发** 。

I bought a second-hand **sofa** set last week.

603 沙子   shā zi   **Noun: sand; grit**

zhēn dǎo méi shā zi chuī jìn wǒ de yǎn jīng lǐ le
真 倒 霉 ！ **沙 子** 吹 进 我 的 眼 睛 里 了 ！

So unlucky! The **sand** blew into my eyes!

604 伤　　　　　　shāng　　　**Verb:** to hurt; to wound
Noun: injury

Verb
qiǎng jié fàn yòng dāo shāng le sān gè rén
抢 劫 犯 用 刀 **伤** 了 三 个 人 。
The robber **wounded** three people with a knife.

Noun
shòu hài zhě de shāng yán zhòng ma
受 害 者 的 **伤** 严 重 吗 ？
Were the victim's **injuries** serious?

605 伤心　　　　　shāng xīn　　　**Adjective:** sad

bié shāng xīn tā men de shāng hěn kuài jiù huì huī fù
别 **伤 心** ， 他 们 的 伤 很 快 就 会 恢 复 。
Don't be **sad**, their injuries will heal soon.

606 商品　　　　　shāng pǐn　　　**Noun:** commodity; goods

zhè xiē shāng pǐn dōu shì cóng zhōng guó jìn kǒu de
这 些 **商 品** 都 是 从 中 国 进 口 的 。
These **goods** are all imported from China.

607 商业　　　　　shāng yè　　　**Noun:** business (industry)

wǒ shì zài yì chǎng shāng yè huó dòng shàng rèn shi tā de
我 是 在 一 场 **商 业** 活 动 上 认 识 他 的 。
I came to know him at a **business** event.

608 上来　　　　　shàng lái　　　**Verb:** to come up

kuài shàng lái wǒ men yì qǐ zài shān dǐng pāi zhào
快 **上 来** ， 我 们 一 起 在 山 顶 拍 照 。
Come up quickly, let's take pictures together on the mountain peak.

609 上面　　shàng miàn　　**Noun:** above; on top of

nǐ kàn, tǎ shàng miàn yǒu yì zhī lǎo yīng
你 看， 塔 上 面 有 一 只 老 鹰 。
You see, there is an eagle **on top of** the tower.

610 上去　　shàng qù　　**Verb:** to go up

tǎ tài gāo, wǒ men hěn nán shàng qù
塔 太 高， 我 们 很 难 上 去 。
The tower is too high for us **to go up**.

611 上升　　shàng shēng　　**Verb:** to rise

tīng shuō, fáng dài lì xī zài shàng shēng
听 说， 房 贷 利 息 在 上 升 。
I heard that mortgage rates are **rising**.

612 上衣　　shàng yī　　**Noun:** jacket; upper outer garment

hái zi zài cǎo dì shàng wán de shí hòu, bǎ shàng yī
孩 子 在 草 地 上 玩 的 时 候， 把 上 衣
nòng zāng le
弄 脏 了 。
When the child was playing on the grass, he got his **jacket** dirty.

613 设备　　shè bèi　　**Noun:** equipment

wǒ men gōng sī de xīn shè bèi hěn xiān jìn
我 们 公 司 的 新 设 备 很 先 进 。
Our company's new **equipment** is very advanced.

614 设计　　　　shè jì　　**Verb:** to design
Noun: design

Verb
wǒ xiǎng qǐng zhuān jiā wèi wǒ shè jì hūn shā
我 想 请 专 家 为 我 **设 计** 婚 纱 。
I would like to have an expert **design** a wedding dress for me.

Noun
tā xiàng wǒ tuī jiàn le zhè kuǎn shè jì
他 向 我 推 荐 了 这 款 **设 计** 。
He recommended this **design** to me.

615 设立　　　　shè lì　　**Verb:** to set up

èr shí nián qián shì tā shè lì le xué shēng huì
二 十 年 前 ， 是 他 **设 立** 了 学 生 会 。
Twenty years ago, he was the one who **set up** the student union.

616 社会　　　　shè huì　　**Noun:** society; social

dà xué shēng de shè huì jīng yàn bú gòu
大 学 生 的 **社 会** 经 验 不 够 。
The **social** experience of university students is not enough.

617 身份证　　　　shēn fèn zhèng　　**Noun:** ID card

wǒ de shēn fèn zhèng hé hù zhào dōu zài wén jiàn jiā
我 的 **身 份 证** 和 护 照 都 在 文 件 夹 。
My **ID card** and passport are both in the folder.

618 深　　　　shēn　　**Adjective:** deep

xiǎo xīn zhè tiáo hé de shuǐ hěn shēn
小 心 ， 这 条 河 的 水 很 **深** 。
Be careful, the water in this river is very **deep**.

619 深刻   shēn kè   **Adjective:** profound (memory or expression)

^{wǒ} 我 ^{duì} 对 ^{jiā} 家 ^{xiāng} 乡 ^{de} 的 ^{jì} 记 ^{yì} 忆 ^{réng} 仍 ^{rán} 然 ^{hěn} 很 ^{shēn} **深** ^{kè} **刻** 。

I still have **profound** memories of my hometown.

620 深入   shēn rù   **Adverb:** in depth

^{wǒ} 我 ^{yào} 要 ^{shēn} **深** ^{rù} **入** ^{xué} 学 ^{xí} 习 ^{zhōng} 中 ^{guó} 国 ^{wén} 文 ^{huà} 化 ^{hé} 和 ^{lì} 历 ^{shǐ} 史 。

I want to study Chinese culture and history **in depth**.

621 生   shēng   **Adjective:** unripe; raw
Verb: to give birth

Adj.   ^{wǒ} 我 ^{bù} 不 ^{chī} 吃 ^{shēng} **生** ^{xiāng} 香 ^{jiāo} 蕉 ，^{zhǐ} 只 ^{chī} 吃 ^{shú} 熟 ^{xiāng} 香 ^{jiāo} 蕉 。

I don't eat **unripe** bananas, only ripe bananas.

Verb   ^{wǒ} 我 ^{jiā} 家 ^{de} 的 ^{mǔ} 母 ^{gǒu} 狗 ^{shēng} **生** ^{le} 了 ^{wǔ} 五 ^{zhī} 只 ^{xiǎo} 小 ^{gǒu} 狗 。

Our family's mother dog **gave birth** to five puppies.

622 生产   shēng chǎn   **Verb:** to produce; to manufacture
Noun: production

Verb   ^{gōng} 工 ^{chǎng} 厂 ^{měi} 每 ^{zhōu} 周 ^{kě} 可 ^{yǐ} 以 ^{shēng} **生** ^{chǎn} **产** ^{yī} 一 ^{qiān} 千 ^{jiàn} 件 ^{xù} T恤 。

The factory can **produce** a thousand T-shirts per week.

Noun   ^{tīng} 听 ^{shàng} 上 ^{qù} 去 ^{shēng} **生** ^{chǎn} **产** ^{liàng} 量 ^{dí} 的 ^{què} 确 ^{hěn} 很 ^{gāo} 高 ！

Sounds like the **production** quantity is indeed very high!

623 生存   shēng cún   **Verb:** to survive
Noun: survival

Verb
huán jìng bèi pò huài hòu   yě shēng dòng wù hěn nán
环 境 被 破 坏 后 ， 野 生 动 物 很 难
shēng cún
生 存 。
After the environment is destroyed, it is difficult for wild animals **to survive.**

Noun
bǎo hù huán jìng duì tā men de shēng cún hěn zhòng yào
保 护 环 境 对 它 们 的 生 存 很 重 要 。
Protecting the environment is important for their **survival.**

624 生动   shēng dòng   **Adjective:** vivid

nǐ duì diàn yǐng de miáo shù hěn shēng dòng
你 对 电 影 的 描 述 很 生 动 。
Your description of the film is **vivid.**

625 生命   shēng mìng   **Noun:** life
(opposite of death)

xiǎo dòng wù de shēng mìng hěn cuì ruò   yào zhào gù hǎo
小 动 物 的 生 命 很 脆 弱 ， 要 照 顾 好 。
The **lives** of small animals are fragile, so take care of them well.

626 生意   shēng yi   **Noun:** business

tā shì chéng gōng de shēng yi rén   shēng yi yě yuè lái
他 是 成 功 的 生 意 人 ， 生 意 也 越 来
yuè dà
越 大 。
He was a successful **business**man, the **business** is also getting bigger and bigger.

627 生长

shēng zhǎng   **Verb:** to grow (plants)

yīng huā shù **shēng zhǎng** de yǒu diǎn màn
櫻 花 树 **生 长** 得 有 点 慢 。
Cherry blossom trees **grow** a little slowly.

628 声明

shēng míng   **Verb:** to state; to declare
Noun: statement

Verb
wǒ **shēng míng** zhèng fǔ bù róng rěn huì lù
我 **声 明** 政 府 不 容 忍 贿 赂 。
I **declare** that the government will not tolerate bribery.

Noun
zhè fèn **shēng míng** de yǐng xiǎng bú tài dà
这 份 **声 明** 的 影 响 不 太 大 。
The **statement** didn't have much impact.

629 胜

shèng   **Verb:** to win

zhè chǎng bǐ sài wǒ **shèng** le tā bài le
这 场 比 赛 ， 我 **胜** 了 ， 他 败 了 。
In this competition, I **won** and he lost.

630 胜利

shèng lì   **Verb:** to win
Noun: victory

Verb
zhōng yú **shèng lì** le ! gān bēi !
终 于 **胜 利** 了 ！ 干 杯 ！
Finally **won**! Cheers!

Noun
shèng lì hé shī bài duì tā hěn zhòng yào ma
胜 利 和 失 败 对 他 很 重 要 吗 ？
Are **victories** and defeats important to him?

631 失去

shī qù   **Verb:** to lose

tā méi yǒu **shī qù** fěn sī de zhī chí
他 没 有 **失 去** 粉 丝 的 支 持 。
He hasn't **lost** the support of his fans.

632 石头　　shí tou　　**Noun:** stone; rock

wǒ de gǒu míng zì shì dà shí tou
我 的 狗 名 字 是 大 **石 头** 。
My dog's name is Big **Stone**.

633 石油　　shí yóu　　**Noun:** petroleum

hěn duō dà de shí yóu gōng sī zài zhōng dōng
很 多 大 的 **石 油** 公 司 在 中 东 。
Many big **petroleum** companies are in the Middle East.

634 时　　shí　　**Noun:** time
(use with other words)

lǎo shī ràng wǒ àn shí jiāo zuò yè
老 师 让 我 **按 时** 交 作 业 。
The teacher asked me to hand in my homework **on time**.

635 时代　　shí dài　　**Noun:** era

lǐ xiǎo lóng shì yí gè shí dài de wǔ shù chuán qí
李 小 龙 是 一 个 **时 代** 的 武 术 传 奇 。
Bruce Lee was a martial arts legend of an **era**.

636 时刻　　shí kè　　**Noun:** point of time;
moment
Adverb: constantly

Noun
zài guān jiàn shí kè tā men de qiú duì jìn qiú le
在 关 键 **时 刻** ，他 们 的 球 队 进 球 了 ！
At the critical **moment**, their football team scored a goal!

Adv.
méi bì yào shí kè tí xǐng tā chī yào
没 必 要 **时 刻** 提 醒 他 吃 药 。
There is no need to remind him to take medicine **constantly**.

637 实际上　shí jì shàng　**Adverb:** in fact; actually

shí jì shàng tā qù nián jiù jiè yān le
实际上，他去年就戒烟了。
In fact, he quit smoking last year.

638 实力　shí lì　**Noun:** strength; ability

bú yào dī gū duì shǒu de shí lì
不要低估对手的实力。
Do not underestimate the **strength** of your opponent.

639 实行　shí xíng　**Verb:** to implement

gōng sī kāi shǐ shí xíng jiǎng jīn zhì dù
公司开始实行奖金制度。
The company began **to implement** a bonus system.

640 实验　shí yàn　**Noun:** experiment

shí yàn de jié guǒ chū lái le ma
实验的结果出来了吗？
Are the results of the **experiment** out?

641 实验室　shí yàn shì　**Noun:** laboratory

kē xué jiā men hái zài shí yàn shì guān chá
科学家们还在实验室观察。
Scientists are still observing in the **laboratory**.

642 食品　shí pǐn　**Noun:** food (product)

zhèng fǔ hěn kàn zhòng shí pǐn ān quán
政府很看重食品安全。
The government regards **food** safety as very important.

643 使   shǐ   **Verb:** to make (formal)

zhè tiáo fǎ lǜ néng shǐ shēng chǎn shāng gèng pèi hé
这 条 法 律 能 **使** 生 产 商 更 配 合 。
This law can **make** manufacturers more cooperative.

644 始终   shǐ zhōng   **Adverb:** throughout

tā men de xié shāng shǐ zhōng méi yǒu jié guǒ
他 们 的 协 商 **始 终** 没 有 结 果 。
They haven't reached a result **throughout** their negotiations.

645 世纪   shì jì   **Noun:** century

èr shí yī shì jì shì hù lián wǎng shí dài
二 十 一 **世 纪** 是 互 联 网 时 代 。
The 21st **century** is the age of the Internet.

646 世界   shì jiè   **Noun:** world

tā shì shì jiè shàng zuì bàng de zú qiú yùn dòng yuán
他 是 **世 界** 上 最 棒 的 足 球 运 动 员 。
He is the best football player in the **world**.

647 世界杯   shì jiè bēi   **Noun:** World Cup

nǐ qī dài xià yí cì shì jiè bēi bǐ sài ma
你 期 待 下 一 次 **世 界 杯** 比 赛 吗 ？
Are you looking forward to the next **World Cup** match?

648 市场   shì chǎng   **Noun:** market

wǒ men yào bǎ chǎn pǐn tuī guǎng dào guó jì shì chǎng
我 们 要 把 产 品 推 广 到 国 际 **市 场** 。
We need to promote our products to the international **market**.

649 事故 — shì gù

Noun: accident (injury related)

警察 在 前 面 调 查 交 通 **事 故** 。
jǐng chá zài qián miàn diào chá jiāo tōng shì gù

Police officers are investigating a traffic **accident** ahead.

650 事件 — shì jiàn

Noun: matter; incident

这 个 **事 件** 引 起 了 严 重 的 堵 车 。
zhè gè shì jiàn yǐn qǐ le yán zhòng de dǔ chē

The **incident** caused severe traffic jams.

651 事实 — shì shí

Noun: fact

很 多 假 新 闻 都 不 报 道 **事 实** 。
hěn duō jiǎ xīn wén dōu bú bào dào shì shí

A lot of fake news doesn't report the **facts**.

652 事实上 — shì shí shàng

Adverb: in fact; actually

事 实 上 ， 很 多 网 民 都 知 道 这 个 。
shì shí shàng hěn duō wǎng mín dōu zhī dào zhè gè

In fact, many netizens know this.

653 事业 — shì yè

Noun: career

在 **事 业 上** ， 他 是 个 非 常 成 功 的 人 。
zài shì yè shàng tā shì gè fēi cháng chéng gōng de rén

In **career**, he is a very successful person.

654 试题 — shì tí

Noun: questions (exams)

这 次 考 试 的 **试 题** 不 太 难 。
zhè cì kǎo shì de shì tí bú tài nán

This time the exam **questions** are not too difficult.

655 试验　　　shì yàn　　　**Noun:** experiment; test (scientific)

每次发射火箭前，他们都要做试验。
měi cì fā shè huǒ jiàn qián, tā men dōu yào zuò shì yàn
Before every rocket launch, they have to do **experiments**.

656 适合　　　shì hé　　　**Verb:** to fit

我觉得这份工作很适合他。
wǒ jué de zhè fèn gōng zuò hěn shì hé tā
I think the job really **fits** him.

657 适应　　　shì yìng　　　**Verb:** to adapt

因为他适应新环境非常快。
yīn wèi tā shì yīng xīn huán jìng fēi cháng kuài
Because he **adapts** to the new environment very quickly.

658 适用　　　shì yòng　　　**Adjective:** applicable

你觉得经理的提议适用吗？
nǐ jué de jīng lǐ de tí yì shì yòng ma
Do you think the manager's proposal is **applicable**?

659 室　　　shì　　　**Noun:** room

这边是卧室，那边是浴室。
zhè biān shì wò shì, nà biān shì yù shì
Here's the bed**room**, there's the bath**room**.

660 收费   shōu fèi   **Verb:** to collect fees; to charge

这 个 停 车 场 **收 费** 太 高 ， 每 小 时
zhè gè tíng chē chǎng shōu fèi tài gāo   měi xiǎo shí

十 美 元 ！
shí měi yuán

This car park **charges** too much, ten dollars an hour!

---

661 收看   shōu kàn   **Verb:** to watch (TV)

你 可 以 在 2 频 道 **收 看** 奥 运 会 比 赛 。
nǐ kě yǐ zài   pín dào shōu kàn ào yùn huì bǐ sài

You can **watch** the Olympic games on Channel 2.

---

662 收听   shōu tīng   **Verb:** to listen to (radio)

爷 爷 总 是 准 时 **收 听** 新 闻 广 播 。
yé ye zǒng shì zhǔn shí shōu tīng xīn wén guǎng bō

Grandpa always **listens to** the news broadcast on time.

---

663 收音机   shōu yīn jī   **Noun:** radio

他 的 **收 音 机** 又 旧 又 破 。
tā de shōu yīn jī yòu jiù yòu pò

His **radio** is old and broken.

---

664 手续   shǒu xù   **Noun:** procedures

我 听 说 办 工 作 签 的 **手 续** 很 复 杂 。
wǒ tīng shuō bàn gōng zuò qiān de shǒu xù hěn fù zá

I heard that the **procedures** for applying for a work visa are very complicated.

665 手指　　shǒu zhǐ　**Noun:** finger

请 别 用 **手 指** 对 着 别 人 ， 不 太 礼 貌 。
qǐng bié yòng shǒu zhǐ duì zhe bié rén bú tài lǐ mào
Please don't point your **fingers** at others, it's not polite.

666 首都　　shǒu dū　**Noun:** capital

美 国 的 **首 都** 是 华 盛 顿 。
měi guó de shǒu dū shì huá shèng dùn
The **capital** of the United States is Washington (D.C.).

667 首先　　shǒu xiān　**Adverb:** firstly

首 先 ， 请 欢 迎 陈 先 生 给 我 们 演 讲 。
shǒu xiān qǐng huān yíng chén xiān shēng gěi wǒ men yǎn jiǎng
Firstly, please welcome Mr. Chen to give us a speech.

668 受　　shòu　**Verb:** to bear; to suffer

他 实 习 的 时 候 ， **受** 了 老 板 的 欺 负 。
tā shí xí de shí hòu shòu le lǎo bǎn de qī fù
During his internship, he **suffered** bullying from his boss.

669 受伤　　shòu shāng　**Verb:** to injure

她 跳 舞 的 时 候 ， 左 脚 **受 伤** 了 。
tā tiào wǔ de shí hòu zuǒ jiǎo shòu shāng le
When she was dancing, her left foot was **injured**.

670 书架　　shū jià　**Noun:** bookshelf

我 的 中 文 书 在 **书 架** 右 边 。
wǒ de zhōng wén shū zài shū jià yòu biān
My Chinese books are on the right side of the **bookshelf**.

671 输   shū   **Verb:** to lose

zhè chǎng bǐ sài wǒ men bù néng shū yí dìng yào yíng
这 场 比 赛 ， 我 们 不 能 输 ， 一 定 要 赢 。
In this competition, we cannot **lose**, we must win.

672 输入   shū rù   **Verb:** to input; to type

wǒ kě yǐ zài shǒu jī shàng shū rù zhōng wén
我 可 以 在 手 机 上 输 入 中 文 。
I can **type** Chinese on my phone.

673 熟人   shú rén   **Noun:** acquaintance

wǒ de lín jū men dōu shì wǒ de shú rén
我 的 邻 居 们 都 是 我 的 熟 人 。
My neighbors are all my **acquaintances**.

674 属   shǔ   **Verb:** be born in the (zodiac) year of

wǒ shǔ lóng nǐ ne
我 属 龙 ， 你 呢 ？
I was **born in the year of** dragon, what about you?

675 属于   shǔ yú   **Verb:** to belong to

bù guǎn guò qù duō jiǔ wǒ de xīn dōu shǔ yú nǐ
不 管 过 去 多 久 ， 我 的 心 都 属 于 你 。
No matter how long has passed, my heart always **belongs to** you.

676 束   shù   **Verb:** to bind; to tie
Classifier: bunch of

Verb

wǒ xǐ huān yòng fà quān shù tóu fa
我 喜 欢 用 发 圈 **束** 头 发 。
I like **to tie** my hair with scrunchies.

Class.

wǒ dǎ suàn gěi tā mǎi yí shù hóng méi guī
我 打 算 给 她 买 一 **束** 红 玫 瑰 。
I'm going to buy her a **bunch of** red roses.

677 数量   shù liàng   **Noun:** quantity

wǒ jué de zhì liàng bǐ shù liàng gèng zhòng yào
我 觉 得 质 量 比 **数 量** 更 重 要 。
I think quality is more important than **quantity**.

678 双   shuāng   **Adjective:** double
Classifier: pair of

Adj.

duì yú zhōng fāng shí xiàn shuāng yíng shì mù biāo
对 于 中 方 ， 实 现 **双** 赢 是 目 标 。
For China's side, achieving a win-win (**double** win) is the goal.

Class.

wǒ zài wǎng shàng mǎi le yì shuāng qiú xié
我 在 网 上 买 了 一 **双** 球 鞋 。
I bought a **pair of** sneakers online.

679 双方   shuāng fāng   **Noun:** both sides

wǒ xī wàng shuāng fāng de hé zuò shùn lì
我 希 望 **双 方** 的 合 作 顺 利 。
I hope the cooperation between **both sides** goes smoothly.

680 思想   sī xiǎng   **Noun:** thought; thinking

wǒ fù mǔ de sī xiǎng yǒu diǎn bǎo shǒu
我 父 母 的 **思 想** 有 点 保 守 。
My parents were a bit conservative in their **thinking**.

681 死　　sǐ　　**Verb:** to die

tā shēng yú nián sǐ yú nián
他 生 于 1950 年， **死** 于 2023 年。
He was born in 1950 and **died** in 2023.

682 速度　　sù dù　　**Noun:** speed

zài gāo sù gōng lù shàng kāi chē yào kòng zhì sù dù
在 高 速 公 路 上 开 车， 要 控 制 **速 度**。
When driving on the highway, control the **speed**.

683 随　　suí　　**Verb:** to follow; to come along

qǐng dài shàng mén piào suí wǒ jìn rù bó wù guǎn
请 带 上 门 票， **随** 我 进 入 博 物 馆。
Please bring your tickets and **follow** me into the museum.

684 所　　suǒ　　**Classifier** for place or spot

wǒ jiā fù jìn yǒu yì suǒ yī yuàn hé yì suǒ xué xiào
我 家 附 近 有 一 **所** 医 院 和 一 **所** 学 校。
There is **a** hospital and **a** school nearby my house.

685 所长　　suǒ zhǎng　　**Noun:** superintendent

tā shì pài chū suǒ de suǒ zhǎng
他 是 派 出 所 的 **所 长**。
He is the **superintendent** of the police station.

686 台　　tái　　**Noun:** platform; desk

wǒ men qù qián tái bàn lǐ rù zhù ba
我 们 去 前 **台** 办 理 入 住 吧。
Let's check in at the front **desk**.

687 谈(话)

tán huà

Verb: to talk; to discuss
Noun: discussion

Verb
老板 和 客户 在 办公室 谈(话)。
lǎo bǎn hé kè hù zài bàn gōng shì tán huà
The boss is **talking** with the client in office.

Noun
我 不 小心 听 到 了 他们 的 谈话。
wǒ bù xiǎo xīn tīng dào le tā men de tán huà
I accidentally overheard their **discussion**.

688 谈判

tán pàn

Verb: to negotiate
Noun: negotiation

Verb
他们 在 谈判 一个 合同。
tā men zài tán pàn yí gè hé tóng
They are **negotiating** a contract.

Noun
我 希望 他们 的 谈判 快点 成功。
wǒ xī wàng tā men de tán pàn kuài diǎn chéng gōng
I wish their **negotiations** a speedy success.

689 汤

tāng

Noun: soup

我 喜欢 喝 番茄 鸡蛋 汤。
wǒ xǐ huān hē fān qié jī dàn tāng
I like to drink tomato and egg **soup**.

690 糖

táng

Noun: sugar

我 喜欢 喝 白 咖啡，每次 都 加 糖。
wǒ xǐ huān hē bái kā fēi měi cì dōu jiā táng
I like to drink white coffee, and always add **sugar** every time.

691 特色

tè sè

Noun: characteristic (of something)

发 红包 是 春节 的 特色。
fā hóng bāo shì chūn jié de tè sè
Sending red packets is a **characteristic** of the Spring Festival.

692 提前   tí qián   **Adverb:** in advance

<small>wèi le qìng zhù shēng rì wǒ tí qián qǐng le jià qī</small>
为 了 庆 祝 生 日 ， 我 提 前 请 了 假 期 。
To celebrate my birthday, I asked for a vacation **in advance**.

693 提问   tí wèn   **Verb:** to raise questions

<small>huān yíng dà jiā zài huì yì shàng tí wèn</small>
欢 迎 大 家 在 会 议 上 提 问 。
Please feel welcome **to raise questions** at the meeting.

694 题目   tí mù   **Noun:** subject (academic)

<small>tā de lùn wén tí mù shì yǒu qíng yǔ ài qíng</small>
他 的 论 文 题 目 是 友 情 与 爱 情 。
The **subject** of his thesis was Friendship and Romantic Love.

695 体会   tǐ huì   **Verb:** to feel; to experience

<small>nǐ néng tǐ huì wǒ nèi xīn de zhēng zhá ma</small>
你 能 体 会 我 内 心 的 挣 扎 吗 ？
Can you **feel** my inner struggle?

696 体现   tǐ xiàn   **Verb:** to reveal; to show

<small>rú guǒ nǐ néng jiù tǐ xiàn nǐ zài hū wǒ</small>
如 果 你 能 ， 就 体 现 你 在 乎 我 。
If you can, then it **shows** that you care about me.

697 体验   tǐ yàn   **Verb:** to experience (physical)
Noun: experience

Verb

wǒ yào dài hái zi qù tǐ yàn huá xuě
我 要 带 孩 子 去 **体 验** 滑 雪 。
I want to take my kids **to experience** skiing.

Noun

zhè cì tǐ yàn zhēn de shì yí gè jīng xǐ
这 次 **体 验** 真 的 是 一 个 惊 喜 ！
The **experience** is truly a great surprise!

698 天空   tiān kōng   **Noun:** sky

zuó wǎn wǒ mèng dào fēi xiàng le tiān kōng
昨 晚 我 梦 到 飞 向 了 **天 空** 。
Last night I dreamed that I flew into the **sky**.

699 甜   tián   **Adjective:** sweet

zhè bēi jī wěi jiǔ bú gòu tián
这 杯 鸡 尾 酒 不 够 **甜** ！
This cocktail is not **sweet** enough!

700 调   tiáo   **Verb:** to mix; to adjust

wǒ xiǎng zài jiǔ lǐ jiā diǎn táng tiáo yí xià wèi dào
我 想 在 酒 里 加 点 糖 ， **调** 一 下 味 道 。
I want to add some sugar to the wine to **adjust** the taste a bit.

701 调整   tiáo zhěng   **Verb:** to adjust
Noun: adjustment

Verb

lǎo bǎn shàng gè zhōu tiáo zhěng le bù mén de jié gòu
老 板 上 个 周 **调 整** 了 部 门 的 结 构 。
The boss **adjusted** the structure of the department last week.

Noun

hěn duō yuán gōng duì zhè cì tiáo zhěng bù mǎn yì
很 多 员 工 对 这 次 **调 整** 不 满 意 。
Many employees were dissatisfied with the **adjustment**.

702 跳　　　　tiào　　　　**Verb:** to jump; to leap; to bounce

wǒ de gǒu xǐ huān tiào lái tiào qù
我 的 狗 喜 欢 **跳** 来 **跳** 去 。
My dog loves to **jump** up and down.

703 跳高　　　　tiào gāo　　　　**Verb:** to jump high

yùn dòng yuán men zài liàn xí tiào gāo
运 动 员 们 在 练 习 **跳** **高** 。
Athletes are practicing **high jump**.

704 跳舞　　　　tiào wǔ　　　　**Verb:** to dance

tā tiào wǔ de shí hòu, kù zi tū rán diào le
他 **跳** **舞** 的 时 候 ， 裤 子 突 然 掉 了 。
When he was **dancing**, his pants suddenly fell off.

705 跳远　　　　tiào yuǎn　　　　**Verb:** to long jump

wǒ gē fēi cháng shàn cháng tiào yuǎn
我 哥 非 常 擅 长 **跳** **远** 。
My older brother is very good at **long jump**.

706 铁　　　　tiě　　　　**Noun:** iron

tīng shuō wǒ men de xīn zhǔ guǎn shì yí wèi tiě niáng zi
听 说 我 们 的 新 主 管 是 一 位 **铁** 娘 子 。
I heard that our new director is an **Iron** Lady.

707 铁路　　　　tiě lù　　　　**Noun:** railway; railroad

zhèng fǔ dǎ suàn chóu qián xiū tiě lù
政 府 打 算 筹 钱 修 **铁** **路** 。
The government intends to raise money to build the **railway**.

708 听力   tīng lì   **Noun:** listening comprehension; hearing

wǒ měi tiān liàn xí zhōng wén tīng lì bàn xiǎo shí
我 每 天 练 习 中 文 **听 力** 半 小 时 。
I practice Chinese **listening** for half an hour every day.

709 听众   tīng zhòng   **Noun:** audience (listeners)

yīn yuè huì de tīng zhòng dà gài yǒu yī qiān rén
音 乐 会 的 **听 众** 大 概 有 一 千 人 。
The concert **audience** was about a thousand people.

710 停止   tíng zhǐ   **Verb:** to stop; to cease

yīn yuè tíng zhǐ le kě shì wǒ réng rán hěn táo zuì
音 乐 **停 止** 了 ， 可 是 我 仍 然 很 陶 醉 。
The music **stopped**, but I was still very intoxicated.

711 通常   tōng cháng   **Adverb:** usually

wǒ tōng cháng měi zhōu liù gěi wǒ de fù mǔ dǎ diàn huà
我 **通 常** 每 周 六 给 我 的 父 母 打 电 话 。
I **usually** call my parents every Saturday.

712 通信   tōng xìn   **Verb:** correspond; to communicate
Noun: correspondence

Verb
wǒ gēn qián nán yǒu hěn jiǔ méi tōng xìn le
我 跟 前 男 友 很 久 没 **通 信** 了 。
I haven't **corresponded** with my ex-boyfriend for a long time.

Noun
wǒ men de tōng xìn yǐ jīng duàn le
我 们 的 **通 信** 已 经 断 了 。
Our **correspondence** has been cut off.

713 同意   tóng yì   **Verb:** to agree

太好了！我妈同意我去中国留学了。
Awesome! My mother **agreed** for me to study in China.

714 痛   tòng   **Adjective:** sore; painful

分手的那天，我的心很痛。
On the day we broke up, my heart was very **painful**.

715 痛(苦)   tòng kǔ   **Noun:** pain

可惜，他体会不到我的痛苦。
Unfortunately, he can't feel my **pain**.

716 头   tóu   **Noun:** leader; head

其实，我们部门的头没有能力。
In fact, the **head** of our department has no ability.

717 头脑   tóu nǎo   **Noun:** mind; brain

也许，他的头脑不够聪明。
Maybe, his **mind** is not smart enough.

718 突出   tū chū   **Adjective:** outstanding

他的演讲非常突出！
His presentation was **outstanding**!

719 突然   tū rán   **Adverb:** suddenly

wǒ tū rán dù zi bù shū fu yào xiū xi yí xià
我 **突 然** 肚 子 不 舒 服， 要 休 息 一 下。

I **suddenly** have an uncomfortable stomach and need to take a break.

720 图(画)   tú huà   **Noun:** drawing; picture

zhè xiē tú huà dōu shì zài wǎng shàng xià zǎi de
这 些 **图 画** 都 是 在 网 上 下 载 的。

These **pictures** are downloaded from the Internet.

721 土   tǔ   **Noun:** soil; earth; dirt

wǒ de gǒu zài huā yuán lǐ páo tǔ
我 的 狗 在 花 园 里 刨 **土**。

My dog is digging **dirt** in the garden.

722 团结   tuán jié   **Adjective:** united

gōng sī de yuán gōng men hěn tuán jié jiù xiàng yì jiā rén
公 司 的 员 工 们 很 **团 结**， 就 像 一 家 人。

The employees of the company are very **united**, like a family.

723 团(体)   tuán tǐ   **Noun:** group

wǒ wèi wǒ men de tuán tǐ gǎn dào jiāo ào
我 为 我 们 的 **团 体** 感 到 骄 傲！

I feel proud of our **group**!

724 推动   tuī dòng   **Verb:** to push forward (metaphorically)

lǐng dǎo men zhǔn bèi tuī dòng jīng jì gǎi gé
领 导 们 准 备 **推 动** 经 济 改 革。

Leaders are ready to **push forward** economic reforms.

725 推广   tuī guǎng

Verb: to promote; to extend
Noun: promotion

Verb
wǒ men de mù biāo shì bǎ chǎn pǐn tuī guǎng dào guó
我 们 的 目 标 是 把 产 品 **推 广** 到 国
jì shì chǎng
际 市 场 。

Our goal is **to promote** our products to the international market.

Noun
zhāng wén fù zé chǎn pǐn de tuī guǎng gōng zuò
张 文 负 责 产 品 的 **推 广** 工 作 。

Zhang Wen is responsible for product **promotion** work.

726 推进   tuī jìn

Verb: to advance; to carry forward

tuī jìn jīng jì fā zhǎn hěn zhòng yào
推 进 经 济 发 展 很 重 要 。

It is important **to advance** economic development.

727 推开   tuī kāi

Verb: to push away

nà gè nán de tū rán tuī kāi le wǒ hěn bù
那 个 男 的 突 然 **推 开** 了 我 , 很 不
lǐ mào
礼 貌 !

That man suddenly **pushed** me **away**, very rude!

728 退   tuì

Verb: to retreat

shì jìn hái shì tuì wǒ men tóu piào jué dìng ba
是 进 , 还 是 **退** , 我 们 投 票 决 定 吧 。

Whether to advance or **retreat**, let's vote to decide.

729 退出   tuì chū

Verb: to withdraw; to quit; to drop out

tīng shuō tā xuān bù tuì chū le dà xuǎn
听 说 , 他 宣 布 **退 出** 了 大 选 。

I heard that he announced he is **withdrawing** from the general election.

730 退休　　　tuì xiū　　　**Verb:** to retire

wǒ bà huì zài liù shí wǔ suì de shí hòu tuì xiū
我 爸 会 在 六 十 五 岁 的 时 候 **退 休** 。
My dad will **retire** at sixty-five.

731 外交　　　wài jiāo　　　**Noun:** diplomacy

wǒ de nán péng yǒu shì gāo jí wài jiāo guān
我 的 男 朋 友 是 高 级 **外 交** 官 。
My boyfriend is a senior diplomat (**diplomacy** official).

732 外面　　　wài miàn　　　**Noun:** outside; outdoors

nǐ kàn wài miàn kāi shǐ xià dà xuě le
你 看 ， **外 面** 开 始 下 大 雪 了 。
You see, it's starting to snow heavily **outside**.

733 外文　　　wài wén　　　**Noun:** foreign language

tā zhǎng wò le liù mén wài wén zhēn shì tiān cái
他 掌 握 了 六 门 **外 文** ， 真 是 天 才 ！
He has mastered six **foreign languages**, what a genius!

734 完美　　　wán měi　　　**Adjective:** perfect
　　　　　　　　　　　　　　　　　　　　Noun: perfection

Adj.
nǐ jué de shì jiè shàng yǒu wán měi de rén ma
你 觉 得 世 界 上 有 **完 美** 的 人 吗 ？
Do you think there are **perfect** people in the world?

Noun
tā shì gè wán měi zhǔ yì zhě
他 是 个 **完 美** 主 义 者 。
He is a **perfection**ist.

735 完善   wán shàn   **Verb:** to refine

wǒ men xū yào wán shàn zhè gè xiàng mù
我 们 需 要 **完 善** 这 个 项 目 。
We need **to refine** this project.

736 完整   wán zhěng   **Adjective:** complete

shì wǒ de ài rén ràng wǒ de shēng mìng wán zhěng
是 我 的 爱 人 让 我 的 生 命 **完 整** ！
It is my spouse who makes my life **complete**!

737 玩具   wán jù   **Noun:** toys

wǒ de nǚ ér zài shèng dàn jié shōu dào le hěn duō
我 的 女 儿 在 圣 诞 节 收 到 了 很 多
wán jù
玩 具 。
My daughter received a lot of **toys** for Christmas.

738 往往   wǎng wǎng   **Adverb:** tend to; often (for a reason)

tā wǎng wǎng gěi tè bié xǐ huān de lǐ wù qǔ míng zì
她 **往 往** 给 特 别 喜 欢 的 礼 物 取 名 字 。
She **tends to** name gifts she particularly likes.

739 危害   wēi hài   **Noun:** harm

xù jiǔ duì shēn tǐ de wēi hài hěn dà
酗 酒 对 身 体 的 **危 害** 很 大 。
Alcoholism is very harmful (**harm** big) to the body.

740 危险　　wēi xiǎn

Adjective: dangerous
Noun: danger

Adj.

zhè lǐ shì xuán yá　zhàn zài shàng miàn hěn wēi xiǎn
这 里 是 悬 崖 ， 站 在 上 面 很 危 险 。
This is a cliff, it's **dangerous** to stand on it.

Noun

tā dǎn dà　bú pà wēi xiǎn
他 胆 大 ， 不 怕 危 险 。
He is bold, not afraid of **danger**

741a 为　　wéi

Verb: to be; to become

wǒ men tóu piào xuǎn le wáng xiān shēng wéi tuán duì lǐng dǎo
我 们 投 票 选 了 王 先 生 为 团 队 领 导 。
We voted Mr. Wang **to be** team leader.

741b 为　　wèi

Preposition: for

gōng sī yǐ jīng wèi tā zhǔn bèi le bàn gōng shì
公 司 已 经 为 他 准 备 了 办 公 室 。
The company has already prepared an office **for** him.

742 围　　wéi

Verb: to surround; to circle

wǒ zuó tiān zǎo shàng wéi hú pǎo le yì quān
我 昨 天 早 上 围 湖 跑 了 一 圈 。
I ran **around** the lake yesterday morning.

743 伟大　　wěi dà

Adjective: great (mighty)

tā shì měi guó lì shǐ shàng wěi dà de zǒng tǒng
他 是 美 国 历 史 上 伟 大 的 总 统 。
He is a **great** president in American history.

744 卫生   wèi shēng   **Noun:** hygiene; sanitation

wǒ men de chǎn pǐn fú hé wèi shēng biāo zhǔn
我 们 的 产 品 符 合 卫 生 标 准 。
Our products meet **hygiene** standards.

745 卫生间   wèi shēng jiān   **Noun:** toilet

qǐng wèn fù jìn yǒu wèi shēng jiān ma
请 问 ， 附 近 有 卫 生 间 吗 ？
Excuse me, is there a **toilet** nearby?

746 为了   wèi le   **Preposition:** for the purpose of; in order to

wèi le zhèng qián tā tóng shí zuò liǎng fèn gōng zuò
为 了 挣 钱 ， 他 同 时 做 两 份 工 作 。
In order to earn money, he worked two jobs at the same time.

747 温暖   wēn nuǎn   **Verb:** to warm / **Adjective:** warm

Verb
tā de shàn liáng wēn nuǎn le wǒ de xīn
她 的 善 良 温 暖 了 我 的 心 。
Her kindness **warmed** my heart.

Adj.
chūn tiān de yáng guāng yòu měi yòu wēn nuǎn
春 天 的 阳 光 又 美 又 温 暖 。
The spring sunshine is beautiful and **warm**.

748 文化   wén huà   **Noun:** culture

wǒ xǐ huān xué xí zhōng guó de lì shǐ hé wén huà
我 喜 欢 学 习 中 国 的 历 史 和 文 化 。
I like learning about Chinese history and **culture**.

749 文件 wén jiàn **Noun:** document; file

wǒ zài sǎo miáo hù zhào hé qiān zhèng wén jiàn
我 在 扫 描 护 照 和 签 证 **文 件** 。
I am scanning passport and visa **documents**.

750 文明 wén míng **Noun:** civilization

wǒ duì xiàn dài wén míng de fā zhǎn yǒu xìng qù
我 对 现 代 **文 明** 的 发 展 有 兴 趣 。
I am interested in the development of modern **civilization**.

751 文学 wén xué **Noun:** literature

wǒ men de jiào shòu shì wén xué zhuān jiā
我 们 的 教 授 是 **文 学** 专 家 。
Our professor is an expert in **literature**.

752 文章 wén zhāng **Noun:** article

tā yǐ jīng fā biǎo le hěn duō xué shù wén zhāng
他 已 经 发 表 了 很 多 学 术 **文 章** 。
He has published many academic **articles**.

753 文字 wén zì **Noun:** script; writing character

wǒ tīng shuō gǔ diǎn wén zì hěn nán kàn dǒng
我 听 说 古 典 **文 字** 很 难 看 懂 。
I've heard that classical **script** is hard to read.

754 握手 wò shǒu **Verb:** to shake hands

tā bù xǐ huān gēn mò shēng rén wò shǒu
他 不 喜 欢 跟 陌 生 人 **握 手** 。
He doesn't like **shaking hands** with strangers.

755 屋子   wū zi   **Noun:** small house; room

zhè jiān wū zi tài lǎo le yīng gāi zhuāng xiū yí xià
这 间 **屋 子** 太 老 了 , 应 该 装 修 一 下 。
This **room** is too old and should be renovated.

756 武器   wǔ qì   **Noun:** weapon

tā gěi wǒ mǎi de wǔ qì shì yì bǎ jiàn
他 给 我 买 的 **武 器** 是 一 把 剑 。
The **weapon** he bought me is a sword.

757 武术   wǔ shù   **Noun:** martial art

wǒ duì zhōng guó wǔ shù fēi cháng gǎn xìng qù
我 对 中 国 **武 术** 非 常 感 兴 趣 。
I am very interested in Chinese **martial arts**.

758 舞台   wǔ tái   **Noun:** stage; arena

kě shì wǒ xué jiàn bú shì wèi le wǔ tái biǎo yǎn
可 是 , 我 学 剑 不 是 为 了 **舞 台** 表 演 。
However, I didn't learn sword for **stage** performance.

759 西部   xī bù   **Noun:** west side

xī zàng zài zhōng guó de xī bù
西 藏 在 中 国 的 **西 部** 。
Tibet is in the **west** (part) of China.

760 希望   xī wàng   **Verb:** to hope
Noun: hope

Verb

^{wǒ}我 ^{xī}希 ^{wàng}望 ^{shuō}说 ^{liú}流 ^{lì}利 ^{de}的 ^{zhōng}中 ^{wén}文 。

I **hope** to speak fluent Chinese.

Noun

^{hái}孩 ^{zi}子 ^{shì}是 ^{guó}国 ^{jiā}家 ^{wèi}未 ^{lái}来 ^{de}的 ^{xī}希 ^{wàng}望 。

Children are the **hope** of the future of the country.

761 系   xì   **Verb:** to tie
Noun: department (academic)

Verb

^{bù}不 ^{hǎo}好 ^{yì}意 ^{si}思 ， ^{wǒ}我 ^{yào}要 ^{xì}系 ^{xié}鞋 ^{dài}带 。

Excuse me, I have **to tie** my shoelaces.

Noun

^{wǒ}我 ^{nǚ}女 ^{péng}朋 ^{yǒu}友 ^{shì}是 ^{shù}数 ^{xué}学 ^{xì}系 ^{de}的 ^{xué}学 ^{shēng}生 。

My girlfriend is a student in the **Department** of Mathematics.

762 下来   xià lái   **Verb:** to come down; to go down

^{lóu}楼 ^{dǐng}顶 ^{hěn}很 ^{wēi}危 ^{xiǎn}险 ， ^{kuài}快 ^{diǎn}点 ^{xià}下 ^{lái}来 。

The roof is dangerous, **come down** quickly.

763 下面   xià miàn   **Noun:** below; underneath

^{zhuō}桌 ^{zi}子 ^{xià}下 ^{miàn}面 ^{yǒu}有 ^{liǎng}两 ^{zhǐ}只 ^{kě}可 ^{ài}爱 ^{de}的 ^{xiǎo}小 ^{māo}猫 。

There are two cute kittens **under** the table.

764 下去 xià qù

Verb: to go down; to descend

我们在山顶拍照，半个小时后会下去。
wǒ men zài shān dǐng pāi zhào, bàn gè xiǎo shí hòu huì xià qù

We are taking pictures at the top of the mountain and will **go down** in half an hour.

765 先进 xiān jìn

Adjective: advanced

人工智能越来越先进。
rén gōng zhì néng yuè lái yuè xiān jìn

Artificial intelligence is more and more **advanced**.

766 显得 xiǎn de

Verb: to appear; to indicate

有时候，我男朋友显得不太在乎我。
yǒu shí hòu, wǒ nán péng yǒu xiǎn de bú tài zài hu wǒ

Sometimes my boyfriend **appears** as if he doesn't care about me that much.

767 显然 xiǎn rán

Adverb: obviously; clearly

我不相信，你显然想太多了！
wǒ bù xiāng xìn, nǐ xiǎn rán xiǎng tài duō le

I don't believe it, you're **clearly** thinking too much!

768 显示 xiǎn shì

Verb: to display

我的电脑屏幕显示快没电了。
wǒ de diàn nǎo píng mù xiǎn shì kuài méi diàn le

My computer screen **displays** that the battery has nearly run out.

769 现场

xiàn chǎng

Noun: site; scene (phyiscal place)

他 们 都 去 了 现 场 排 队 买 票 。
tā men dōu qù le xiàn chǎng pái duì mǎi piào

They all went to the **scene** to line up to buy tickets.

770 现代

xiàn dài

Adjective: modern

现 代 的 生 活 质 量 比 古 代 更 高 。
xiàn dài de shēng huó zhì liàng bǐ gǔ dài gèng gāo

The quality of life in **modern** times is higher than in ancient times.

771 现金

xiàn jīn

Noun: cash

我 没 有 现 金 ， 可 以 刷 卡 吗 ？
wǒ méi yǒu xiàn jīn kě yǐ shuā kǎ ma

I don't have **cash**, can I pay by card?

772 现实

xiàn shí

Noun: reality

保 持 现 实 和 理 想 的 平 衡 很 重 要 。
bǎo chí xiàn shí hé lǐ xiǎng de píng héng hěn zhòng yào

It is important to maintain a balance between **reality** and dreams.

773 现象

xiàn xiàng

Noun: phenomenon

犯 罪 现 象 在 这 个 农 村 不 常 见 。
fàn zuì xiàn xiàng zài zhè gè nóng cūn bù cháng jiàn

Crime **phenomenon** is not common in this village.

774 线

xiàn

Noun: thread; wire; line

让 孩 子 别 碰 ， 那 是 电 线 。
ràng hái zi bié pèng nà shì diàn xiàn

Ask the kids not to touch, that's electic **wire**.

775 相比   xiāng bǐ   **Verb: to compare**

gēn tā xiāng bǐ, wǒ men dōu bú suàn yǒu qián
跟 他 **相 比**，我 们 都 不 算 有 钱 。
Compared to him, we are all not considered rich.

776 相当   xiāng dāng   **Adverb: quite; fairly**

tā shì shì jiè shǒu fù, zài guó jì shàng xiāng dāng
他 是 世 界 首 富，在 国 际 上 **相 当**
yǒu míng
有 名 。
He is the richest man in the world and **quite** famous internationally.

777 相关   xiāng guān   **Adjective: correlate; relevant**

wǒ xǐ huān dú yǔ tóu zī xiāng guān de shū
我 喜 欢 读 与 投 资 **相 关** 的 书 。
I like to read books **related** to investing.

778 相互   xiāng hù   **Adverb: mutual; each other**

zài wǒ men de jī gòu, tóng shì men cháng cháng xiāng hù
在 我 们 的 机 构，同 事 们 常 常 **相 互**
bāng zhù
帮 助 。
In our institution, colleagues often help **each other**.

779 相似   xiāng sì   **Adjective: similar**

nǐ men gōng sī de wén huà hé wǒ men de hěn xiāng sì
你 们 公 司 的 文 化 和 我 们 的 很 **相 似** 。
Your company's culture is very **similar** to ours.

780 香　　　　xiāng　　　Adjective: fragrant

zhè píng xiāng shuǐ de wèi dào fēi cháng xiāng
这 瓶 香 水 的 味 道 非 常 香 。
The scent of this bottle of perfume is very **fragrant**.

781 香蕉　　　xiāng jiāo　　Noun: banana

wǒ měi tiān shàng wǔ dōu chī yí gè xiāng jiāo
我 每 天 上 午 都 吃 一 个 香 蕉 。
I always eat a **banana** every morning.

782 消费　　　xiāo fèi

Verb: to consume
Noun: consumption
(economic activity)

Verb
tā zhè gè zhōu mò xiāo fèi le yī qiān yīng bàng
他 这 个 周 末 消 费 了 一 千 英 镑 。
He **consumed** a thousand pounds this weekend.

Noun
tā de xiāo fèi guān niàn dí què hé wǒ men de bù
他 的 消 费 观 念 的 确 和 我 们 的 不
yí yàng
一 样 。
His view of **consumption** is indeed different from ours.

783 消失　　　xiāo shī　　Verb: to disappear

tā tū rán xiāo shī hòu wǒ jiù bào jǐng le
她 突 然 消 失 后 ， 我 就 报 警 了 。
After she suddenly **disappeared**, I called the police.

784 消息　　　xiāo xi

Noun: news;
message

yǐ jīng sān tiān le wǒ men hái shì méi yǒu tā
已 经 三 天 了 ， 我 们 还 是 没 有 她
de xiāo xi
的 消 息 。
It's been three days and we still haven't heard **news** about her.

785 效果   xiào guǒ   **Noun:** effect

jié shí duì jiǎn féi yǒu xiào guǒ ma
节 食 对 减 肥 有 **效 果** 吗 ？
Is dieting effective (has **effect**) for weight loss?

786 写作   xiě zuò   **Verb:** to write (formal)

wǒ dú bó shì de shí hòu cháng cháng xiě zuò
我 读 博 士 的 时 候 ， 常 常 **写 作** 。
When I was pursuing my Ph.D. degree, I **wrote** a lot.

787 血   xuè   **Noun:** blood

nǐ de shǒu zhǐ shàng yǒu xuè fā shēng shén me le
你 的 手 指 上 有 **血** ， 发 生 什 么 了 ？
You have **blood** on your finger, what happened?

788 心   xīn   **Noun:** heart; core

wǒ de shǒu zhǐ méi shì dàn shì wǒ de xīn zài liú xuè
我 的 手 指 没 事 ， 但 是 我 的 **心** 在 流 血 。
My fingers are fine, but my **heart** is bleeding.

789 信   xìn   **Verb:** to believe
                           Noun: letter; message

Verb
shén me nǐ lǎo gōng chū guǐ le wǒ bú xìn
什 么 ？ 你 老 公 出 轨 了 ？ 我 不 **信** 。
What? Your husband cheated on you? I don't **believe** it.

Noun
wǒ xǐ huān fā duǎn xìn bù xǐ huān xiě xìn
我 喜 欢 发 短 **信** ， 不 喜 欢 写 **信** 。
I like sending text **messages**, but don't like writing **letters**.

790 信封　　　xìn fēng　　**Noun:** envelope

wǒ zài wǎng shàng mǎi le jǐ bāo xìn fēng
我 在 网 上 买 了 几 包 信 封。
I bought several packs of **envelopes** online.

791 信任　　　xìn rèn　　**Verb:** to trust
　　　　　　　　　　　　　　Noun: trust

Verb
nǐ xìn rèn nǐ de hé zuò huǒ bàn ma
你 信 任 你 的 合 作 伙 伴 吗 ？
Do you **trust** your business partners?

Noun
wǒ hěn róng xìng yǒu nǐ de xìn rèn
我 很 荣 幸 有 你 的 信 任 ！
I am honored to have your **trust**!

792 行李　　　xíng li　　**Noun:** luggage;
　　　　　　　　　　　　　　baggage

nín hǎo wǒ yào tuō yùn wǒ de xíng li
您 好 ！ 我 要 托 运 我 的 行 李 。
Hello! I want to check in my **luggage**.

793 形成　　　xíng chéng　　**Verb:** to form
　　　　　　　　　　　　　　　Noun: formation

Verb
pín kùn de jiā tíng bèi jǐng xíng chéng le tā jiān qiáng
贫 困 的 家 庭 背 景 形 成 了 他 坚 强
de xìng gé
的 性 格 。
His poor family background **formed** his strong character.

Noun
xìng gé de xíng chéng yǒu hěn duō yīn sù
性 格 的 形 成 有 很 多 因 素 。
There are many factors in the **formation** of character.

794 形式　　　xíng shì　　**Noun:** formality

kāi mù shì zhǐ shì yí gè xíng shì bú yòng dān xīn
开 幕 式 只 是 一 个 形 式 ， 不 用 担 心 。
The opening ceremony is just a **formality**, don't worry about it.

795 形象   xíng xiàng   **Noun:** image; appearance

_{ài} _{miàn} _{zi} _{de} _{rén} _{dōu} _{hěn} _{zài} _{hu} _{tā} _{men} _{de} _{xíng} _{xiàng}
爱 面 子 的 人 都 很 在 乎 他 们 的 **形 象** 。
Face-saving people really care about their **image**.

796 形状   xíng zhuàng   **Noun:** shape

月 饼 的 **形 状** 一 般 是 圆 形 或 方 形 。
The **shapes** of mooncakes are generally round or square.

797 幸福   xìng fú   **Adjective:** happy (deeply)   **Noun:** happiness

Adj.
我 的 婚 姻 一 直 非 常 **幸 福** 。
My marriage has always been very **happy**.

Noun
你 们 的 **幸 福** 是 我 最 大 的 安 慰 。
Your **happiness** is my greatest comfort.

798 幸运   xìng yùn   **Adjective:** lucky   **Noun:** luck

Adj.
跟 他 结 婚 让 我 觉 得 很 **幸 运** 。
I feel very **lucky** to marry him.

Noun
成 为 你 的 妻 子 是 我 的 **幸 运** 。
It is my **luck** to be your wife.

799 性   xìng

Suffix: nature; gender
Noun: sexuality; sex

Suffix
人 性 很 复 杂 ， 不 管 是 男 性 还 是
女 性 。
rén xìng hěn fù zá   bù guǎn shì nán xìng hái shì
nǚ xìng

Human nature is complex, whether **male** or **female**.

Noun
性 生 活 是 个 人 隐 私 ， 不 要 问 。
xìng shēng huó shì gè rén yǐn sī bú yào wèn

Sex life is a matter of personal privacy, don't ask.

800 性别   xìng bié

Noun: gender

很 多 人 觉 得 改 变 性 别 很 奇 怪 。
hěn duō rén jué de gǎi biàn xìng bié hěn qí guài

Many people find it strange to change gender.

801 性格   xìng gé

Noun:
personal character

我 喜 欢 她 独 立 思 考 的 性 格 。
wǒ xǐ huān tā dú lì sī kǎo de xìng gé

I like her **character** of independent thinking.

802 修   xiū

Verb: to embellish
to repair; to build

我 要 请 人 来 我 家 帮 我 修 冰 箱 。
wǒ yào qǐng rén lái wǒ jiā bāng wǒ xiū bīng xiāng

I'm going to pay someone to come to my house **to repair** my refrigerator.

803 修改   xiū gǎi

Verb: to correct;
to revise

你 可 以 帮 我 修 改 论 文 吗 ？
nǐ kě yǐ bāng wǒ xiū gǎi lùn wén ma

Can you help me **revise** my thesis?

804 需求　　xū qiú　　**Noun:** requirement; demand

请 你 按 照 客 户 的 需 求 发 货 。
qǐng nǐ àn zhào kè hù de xū qiú fā huò
Please ship the goods according to the **requirements** of customers.

805 需要　　xū yào　　**Verb:** to need

我 们 需 要 诚 实 透 明 的 合 作 关 系 。
wǒ men xū yào chéng shí tòu míng de hé zuò guān xi
We **need** honest and transparent partnerships.

806 宣布　　xuān bù　　**Verb:** to announce; to declare

我 宣 布 毕 业 典 礼 现 在 开 始 。
wǒ xuān bù bì yè diǎn lǐ xiàn zài kāi shǐ
I **declare** that graduation ceremonies begin now.

807 宣传　　xuān chuán　　**Verb:** to promote
Noun: promotion

Verb
做 视 频 宣 传 产 品 很 流 行 。
zuò shì pín xuān chuán chǎn pǐn hěn liú xíng
Making videos **to promote** products is very popular.

Noun
什 么 广 告 宣 传 最 有 效 ？
shén me guǎng gào xuān chuán zuì yǒu xiào
What advertising **promotion** is most effective?

808 选手　　xuǎn shǒu　　**Noun:** player

这 位 选 手 才 十 五 岁 ， 真 的 吗 ？
zhè wèi xuǎn shǒu cái shí wǔ suì zhēn de ma
This **player** is only fifteen, really?

809 学费　　xué fèi　　**Noun:** tuition fee; school fee

tīng shuō sī lì xué xiào de **xué fèi** hěn gāo
听 说 私 立 学 校 的 **学 费** 很 高 。
I heard that the **tuition fees** of private schools are very high.

810 训练　　xùn liàn　　**Verb:** to train (physical)
Noun: training

Verb
jiào liàn zài cāo chǎng **xùn liàn** xué yuán
教 练 在 操 场 **训 练** 学 员 。
The coach is **training** the students on the playground.

Noun
zhè cì **xùn liàn** huì chí xù liǎng gè xīng qī
这 次 **训 练** 会 持 续 两 个 星 期 。
This **training** will last for two weeks.

811 压　　yā　　**Verb:** to press; to crush

zāo gāo shū shu de tuǐ bèi chē lún **yā** le
糟 糕 ， 叔 叔 的 腿 被 车 轮 **压** 了 。
Oops, uncle's leg was **crushed** by the wheel.

812 压力　　yā lì　　**Noun:** pressure

tā zuì jìn tiān tiān jiā bān **yā lì** hěn dà
他 最 近 天 天 加 班 ， **压 力** 很 大 。
He has been working overtime every day recently, and is under a lot of **pressure**.

813 烟　　yān　　**Noun:** smoke

wǒ wén dào **yān** le yǒu rén zài fù jìn chōu yān ma
我 闻 到 **烟** 了 ， 有 人 在 附 近 抽 烟 吗 ？
I smell **smoke**, is someone smoking nearby?

814 眼前　　yǎn qián　　**Noun:** right now; before one's eyes; in front

眼 前 最 重 要 的 是 解 决 问 题 。
yǎn qián zuì zhòng yào de shì jiě jué wèn tí

The most important thing **right now** is to solve the problem.

815 演　　yǎn　　**Verb:** to act; to perform

男 主 角 演 得 非 常 好 ！
nán zhǔ jué yǎn de fēi cháng hǎo

The leading actor **acted** very well!

816 演唱　　yǎn chàng　　**Verb:** to sing (performing)

他 今 天 在 舞 台 上 演 唱 了 三 首 歌 。
tā jīn tiān zài wǔ tái shàng yǎn chàng le sān shǒu gē

He **sang** three songs on stage today.

817 演唱会　　yǎn chàng huì　　**Noun:** concert

我 要 坐 飞 机 去 纽 约 参 加 他 的 演 唱 会 。
wǒ yào zuò fēi jī qù niǔ yuē cān jiā tā de yǎn chàng huì

I'm flying to New York to attend his **concert**.

818 演出　　yǎn chū　　**Verb:** to perform　**Noun:** performance

Verb

他 从 小 就 喜 欢 上 台 演 出 。
tā cóng xiǎo jiù xǐ huān shàng tái yǎn chū

He has loved **performing** on stage since he was a child.

Noun

观 众 非 常 期 待 他 的 演 出 。
guān zhòng fēi cháng qī dài tā de yǎn chū

The audience is looking forward to his **performance** very much.

819 演员　　　yǎn yuán　　**Noun:** actor; performer

tā jīn nián huò dé le zuì jiā yǎn yuán jiǎng
他 今 年 获 得 了 最 佳 **演 员** 奖 。
He won the best **actor** award this year.

820 羊　　　yáng　　**Noun:** sheep

nà gè mù yáng rén yǒu shí zhī yáng
那 个 牧 羊 人 有 十 只 **羊** 。
The shepherd had ten **sheep**.

821 阳光　　　yáng guāng　　**Noun:** sunshine

zhè lǐ yáng guāng tài qiáng zuì hǎo dài tài yáng jìng
这 里 **阳 光** 太 强 ， 最 好 戴 太 阳 镜 。
The **sunshine** is too strong here, you'd better wear sunglasses.

822 要是　　　yào shi　　**Conjunction:** if

yào shi pí fū bèi zǐ wài xiàn zhuó shāng jiù bù hǎo
要 是 皮 肤 被 紫 外 线 灼 伤 ， 就 不 好 。
If skin is burned by UV rays, it is not good.

823 衣架　　　yī jià　　**Noun:** hanger; clothes stand

wǒ de xīn yī jià shì kě yǐ zhé dié de
我 的 新 **衣 架** 是 可 以 折 叠 的 。
My new clothes **hanger** is foldable.

824 一切　　　yí qiè　　**Noun:** everything

yào jì zhù qián bù néng mǎi yí qiè
要 记 住 ， 钱 不 能 买 **一 切** 。
Remember, money can't buy **everything**.

825 已(经)   yǐ jīng   **Adverb:** already

fàng xīn, hé tóng wèn tí yǐ jīng jiě jué
放 心 ， 合 同 问 题 已 经 解 决 。
Rest assured, the contract issue has **already** been resolved.

826 以来   yǐ lái   **Noun:** since

jié hūn yǐ lái, wǒ men yì zhí xiāng hù bāo róng
结 婚 以 来 ， 我 们 一 直 相 互 包 容 。
Since we got married, we have always tolerated each other.

827 一方面   yì fāng miàn   **Conjunction:** on one hand

yì fāng miàn wǒ yào tóu zī gǔ shì, lìng yì fāng miàn
一 方 面 我 要 投 资 股 市 ， 另 一 方 面
wǒ yào shěng qián
我 要 省 钱 。
On one hand, I want to invest in the stock market, and **on the other hand**, I need to save money.

828 艺术   yì shù   **Noun:** art

tā zài yì shù fāng miàn shì yí gè tiān cái
她 在 艺 术 方 面 是 一 个 天 才 。
In the aspect of **art**, she is a genius.

829 意外   yì wài   **Noun:** accident

tā de huà huò jiǎng bú shì yí gè yì wài
她 的 画 获 奖 不 是 一 个 意 外 。
It was no **accident** that her painting won the prize.

830 意义　　　yì yì　　　**Noun:** meaning; significance

hǎo de zhōng wén míng zì dōu dài hěn hǎo de yì yì
好 的 中 文 名 字 都 带 很 好 的 **意 义**。
Good Chinese names always carry good **meanings**.

831 因此　　　yīn cǐ　　　**Conjunction:** therefore

yīn cǐ qǔ míng zì bù néng tài suí biàn
因 此， 取 名 字 不 能 太 随 便 。
Therefore picking names should not be too random.

832 银　　　yín　　　**Noun:** silver

wǒ yǒu yí gè jīn jiè zhǐ hé yí gè yín jiè zhǐ
我 有 一 个 金 戒 指 和 一 个 **银** 戒 指 。
I have a gold ring and a **silver** ring.

833 银牌　　　yín pái　　　**Noun:** silver medal

wǒ péng yǒu yíng le ào yùn huì de yín pái
我 朋 友 赢 了 奥 运 会 的 **银 牌** 。
My friend won the **silver medal** in the Olympics.

834 印象　　　yìn xiàng　　　**Noun:** impression

suī rán cái jiàn guò yí cì dàn wǒ duì tā de
虽 然 才 见 过 一 次 ， 但 我 对 他 的
yìn xiàng hěn shēn
印 象 很 深 。
Although I have only met him once, I have a deep **impression** of him.

835 应当　yīng dāng　**Adverb:** should; ought to

tā jué de měi gè rén dōu yīng dāng wú tiáo jiàn bāng tā
他 觉 得 每 个 人 都 应 当 无 条 件 帮 他 。
He feels that everyone **should** help him unconditionally.

836 迎接　yíng jiē　**Verb:** to pick; to welcome

wǒ yào dài biǎo zǒng jīng lǐ qù yíng jiē kè hù
我 要 代 表 总 经 理 去 迎 接 客 户 。
I need to represent the CEO **to welcome** the client.

837 营养　yíng yǎng　**Noun:** nutrition

tā gāng gāng shēng le hái zi xū yào bǔ chōng yíng yǎng
她 刚 刚 生 了 孩 子 ， 需 要 补 充 营 养 。
She just had a baby and needs supplemental **nutrition**.

838 赢　yíng　**Verb:** to win

zài shì jiè bēi zǒng jué sài nǎ gè duì yíng le
在 世 界 杯 总 决 赛 ， 哪 个 队 赢 了 ，
nǎ gè duì shū le
哪 个 队 输 了 ？
In the World Cup finals, which team **won** and which team lost?

839 影视　yǐng shì　**Noun:** film and television

wǒ lǎo gōng zài yǐng shì háng yè gōng zuò
我 老 公 在 影 视 行 业 工 作 。
My husband works in the **film and television** industry.

840 应用

yìng yòng

Verb: to apply
Noun: application

Verb

qǐng jiāo wǒ zěn me yìng yòng zhè gè fāng fǎ jiě jué
请 教 我 怎 么 **应 用** 这 个 方 法 解 决
wèn tí
问 题 。

Please teach me how **to apply** this method to solve the problem.

Noun

duō shù rén dōu bù dǒng zhè gè yìng yòng fāng fǎ
多 数 人 都 不 懂 这 个 **应 用** 方 法 。

Most people don't understand this **application** method.

841 优点

yōu diǎn

Noun: merit; strength

tā de yōu diǎn duō yú tā de quē diǎn
他 的 **优 点** 多 于 他 的 缺 点 。

His **merits** outweigh his demerits.

842 优势

yōu shì

Noun: advantage; strength

měi gè tuán duì dōu yǒu yōu shì hé liè shì
每 个 团 队 都 有 **优 势** 和 劣 势 。

Every team has **strengths** and weaknesses.

843 由

yóu

Preposition: via; under

zhè gè xiàng mù yóu tā fù zé
这 个 项 目 **由** 他 负 责 。

This project is **under** his charge.

844 由于

yóu yú

Preposition: due to

yóu yú gōng zuò yā lì dà tā cháng cháng jiā bān
由 于 工 作 压 力 大 , 他 常 常 加 班 。

Due to the high work pressure, he often works overtime.

845 邮件　　　yóu jiàn　　　**Noun:** email; postal matter

wǒ měi tiān yào chǔ lǐ chà bù duō yī bǎi fēng yóu jiàn
我 每 天 要 处 理 差 不 多 一 百 封 **邮 件** 。
I deal with almost a hundred **emails** a day.

846 邮票　　　yóu piào　　　**Noun:** postage stamp; stamp

wǒ dì xǐ huān shōu jí bù tóng guó jiā de yóu piào
我 弟 喜 欢 收 集 不 同 国 家 的 **邮 票** 。
My younger brother likes to collect **stamps** from different countries.

847 邮箱　　　yóu xiāng　　　**Noun:** postbox; inbox; mailbox

wǒ yǒu gōng zuò yóu xiāng hé gè rén yóu xiāng
我 有 工 作 **邮 箱** 和 个 人 **邮 箱** 。
I have a work **inbox** and a personal **inbox**.

848 游　　　yóu　　　**Verb:** to travel; to tour

wǒ xià gè yuè huì hé péng yǒu men chūn yóu
我 下 个 月 会 和 朋 友 们 春 **游** 。
I will go on a spring **tour** with my friends next month.

849 游戏　　　yóu xì　　　**Noun:** game

yǒu xiē rén bǎ liàn ài dāng chéng yóu xì
有 些 人 把 恋 爱 当 成 **游 戏** 。
Some people treat dating as a **game**.

850 游泳　　　yóu yǒng　　　**Verb:** to swim

wǒ měi zhōu èr wǎn shàng dōu qù yóu yǒng chí yóu yǒng
我 每 周 二 晚 上 都 去 **游 泳** 池 **游 泳** 。
I go **swimming** in the **swimming** pool every Tuesday night.

851 有的是　yǒu de shì　have plenty of; there's no lack of

wǒ mā tuì xiū le， yǒu de shì shí jiān
我 妈 退 休 了 ， **有 的 是** 时 间 。
My mother is retired and **has plenty of** time.

852 有利　yǒu lì　Adjective: favorable; beneficial

duō shuì jiào duì jiàn kāng wú lì， duō yùn dòng cái
多 睡 觉 对 健 康 无 利 ， 多 运 动 才
yǒu lì
有 利 。
Too much sleep is harmful to health, more exercise is **beneficial**.

853 有效　yǒu xiào　Adjective: effective; valid

chī yào wú xiào， bāng tā jiǎn shǎo yā lì cái yǒu xiào
吃 药 无 效 ， 帮 他 减 少 压 力 才 **有 效** 。
Medication is ineffective, helping him to reduce stress is **effective**.

854 预报　yù bào　Noun: prediction; forecast

měi cì chū mén， wǒ dōu huì kàn tiān qì yù bào
每 次 出 门 ， 我 都 会 看 天 气 **预 报** 。
Every time I go out, I always check the weather **forecast**.

855 预防　yù fáng　Verb: to prevent　Noun: prevention

Verb
wǒ men yào yù fáng bìng dú màn yán
我 们 要 **预 防** 病 毒 蔓 延 。
We need **to prevent** the spread of the virus.

Noun
xī wàng zhèng fǔ de yù fáng cuò shī huì yǒu xiào
希 望 政 府 的 **预 防** 措 施 会 有 效 。
Hopefully the government's **prevention** measures will be effective.

856 预计 yù jì **Verb:** to expect; to estimate

wǒ yù jì míng nián sān yuè néng kòng zhì bìng dú
我 预 计 明 年 三 月 能 控 制 病 毒 。
I **expect** that we can control the virus by next March.

857 预习 yù xí **Verb:** to preview

zāo gāo wǒ zuó wǎn wàng jì yù xí kè le
糟 糕 ！ 我 昨 晚 忘 记 预 习 课 了 。
Oops! I forgot **to preview** my lessons last night.

858 员 yuán **Suffix:** a person engaged in professional activity

wǒ jiě shì fú wù yuán wǒ gē shì zhí yuán
我 姐 是 服 务 员 ， 我 哥 是 职 员 。
My older sister is a **waitress** and my older brother is a **clerk**.

859 员工 yuán gōng **Noun:** staff; employee

gōng sī huì bāng yuán gōng mǎi yǎng lǎo bǎo xiǎn ma
公 司 会 帮 员 工 买 养 老 保 险 吗 ？
Will the company buy pension insurance for **employees**?

860 愿望 yuàn wàng **Noun:** wish

nǐ de shēng rì yuàn wàng shì shén me
你 的 生 日 愿 望 是 什 么 ？
What's your birthday **wish**?

861 约　　　　yuē　　　**Verb:** to arrange (appointment)

wǒ xiǎng yuē xiǎo wén yì qǐ qù diàn yǐng yuàn
我 想 **约** 小 文 一 起 去 电 影 院 。
I want to **arrange** (a time) to go to the cinema with Xiaowen together.

862 乐队　　　　yuè duì　　　**Noun:** orchestra; music band

tīng shuō zhè gè yuè duì zài nán měi zhōu fēi cháng yǒu míng
听 说 这 个 **乐队** 在 南 美 洲 非 常 有 名 。
I heard that this **band** is very famous in South America.

863 运输　　　　yùn shū　　　**Verb:** to transport
　　　　　　　　　　　　　　　Noun: transport

Verb
zhè liàng huò chē yùn shū shū cài hé shuǐ guǒ
这 辆 货 车 **运 输** 蔬 菜 和 水 果 。
This truck **transports** vegetables and fruits.

Noun
nǐ men guó jiā de tiě lù yùn shū xì tǒng zěn me yàng
你 们 国 家 的 铁 路 **运 输** 系 统 怎 么 样 ？
How is the rail **transportation** system in your country?

864 杂志　　　　zá zhì　　　**Noun:** magazine

wǒ xiǎng qǔ xiāo wǒ de zá zhì dìng yuè
我 想 取 消 我 的 **杂 志** 订 阅 。
I want to cancel my **magazine** subscription.

865 早已　　　　zǎo yǐ　　　**Adverb:** long ago; for a long time

qí shí wǒ zǎo yǐ duì tā méi gǎn jué le
其 实 ， 我 **早 已** 对 他 没 感 觉 了 。
In fact, I haven't had feelings for him **for a long time**.

866 造   zào   **Verb:** to make; to build

tā zhǔn bèi zào yí jià sī rén fēi jī

他 准 备 **造** 一 架 私 人 飞 机 。
He is going **to build** a private jet.

867 造成   zào chéng   **Verb:** to cause (negative)

dà liàng kǎn shù zào chéng le zhè cì hóng shuǐ

大 量 砍 树 **造 成** 了 这 次 洪 水 。
Large number of felled trees **caused** this flood.

868 责任   zé rèn   **Noun:** responsibility

bǎo hù huán jìng yě shì jū mín de zé rèn

保 护 环 境 也 是 居 民 的 **责 任** 。
Protecting the environment is also the **responsibility** of residents.

869 增加   zēng jiā   **Verb:** to increase; to add

zhèng fǔ yīng gāi zēng jiā bǎo hù cuò shī

政 府 应 该 **增 加** 保 护 措 施 。
The government should **increase** protection measures.

870 增长   zēng zhǎng   **Verb:** to grow; to rise

guó nèi shēng chǎn zǒng zhí bǐ qù nián zēng zhǎng le bǎi

国 内 生 产 总 值 比 去 年 **增 长** 了 百

fēn zhī sān

分 之 三 。
GDP **grew** by 3% over the previous year.

871 展开   zhǎn kāi   **Verb:** to launch; to start (activity)

tóng xué men zhǎn kāi le rè liè de tǎo lùn
同 学 们 **展 开** 了 热 烈 的 讨 论 。
The classmates **started** a lively discussion.

872 张   zhāng   **Classifier** for thin and wide things

wǒ jiàn yì nǐ yòng zhè zhāng zhǐ dǎ yìn
我 建 议 你 用 这 **张** A4 纸 打 印 。
I suggest you print on this **piece** of A4 paper.

873 照   zhào   **Verb:** to reflect; to take (a photo)

kuài bǎi zào xíng wǒ bāng nǐ zhào yì zhāng piào liang
快 摆 造 型 ， 我 帮 你 **照** 一 张 漂 亮
de zhào piàn
的 照 片 。
Quickly do a pose, let me **take** a nice photo for you.

874 者   zhě   **Suffix:** for people

huì yì shàng yǒu xué zhě dú zhě hé zuò zhě
会 议 上 有 **学 者** ， **读 者** 和 **作 者** 。
There are **scholars**, **readers** and **authors** at the conference.

875 真实   zhēn shí   **Adjective:** real; true

jù shuō zhè gè diàn yǐng lái zì yí gè zhēn shí
据 说 ， 这 个 电 影 来 自 一 个 **真 实**
de gù shì
的 故 事 。
It is said that this movie comes from a **true** story.

876 争   zhēng   **Verb:** to contest; to dispute

shén me   liǎng gè nán shēng zài zhēng tóng yí gè nǚ
什 么 ！两 个 男 生 在 **争** 同 一 个 女
péng yǒu
朋 友 ？

What! Two guys are **contesting** over the same girlfriend?

877 争取   zhēng qǔ   **Verb:** to strive for

wǒ yào nǔ lì zhēng qǔ huò dé jīn pái
我 要 努 力 **争 取** 获 得 金 牌 。

I'm going **to strive** hard to get the gold medal.

878 整(个)   zhěng gè   **Adjective:** whole; all; entire

tā zài bàn gōng shì máng le yì zhěng tiān
他 在 办 公 室 忙 了 一 **整** 天 。

He has been busy **whole** day in the office.

tā de zhěng gè shēn tǐ dōu tòng
他 的 **整 个** 身 体 都 痛 。

His **entire** body hurts.

879 整理   zhěng lǐ   **Verb:** to tidy up

kè tīng tài zāng le nǐ kě yǐ zhěng lǐ yí xià ma
客 厅 太 脏 了 ，你 可 以 **整 理** 一 下 吗 ？

The living room is too dirty, can you **tidy** it **up** a bit?

880 整齐   zhěng qí   **Adjective:** neat; organized

nǐ de yī guì kàn shàng qù fēi cháng zhěng qí
你 的 衣 柜 看 上 去 非 常 **整 齐** 。

Your closet looks very **organized**.

881 整体   zhěng tǐ   **Noun:** whole

wǒ men de gōng sī shì yí gè tuán jié de zhěng tǐ
我 们 的 公 司 是 一 个 团 结 的 **整 体** 。
Our company is a united **whole**.

882 整天   zhěng tiān   **Noun:** all day

tā zhěng tiān tǎng zài shā fā shàng kàn diàn shì
他 **整 天** 躺 在 沙 发 上 看 电 视 ！
He lies on the couch watching TV **all day**!

883 整整   zhěng zhěng   **Adjective:** whole; full

tā tǎng zài nà lǐ zhěng zhěng liù gè xiǎo shí le
他 躺 在 那 里 **整 整** 六 个 小 时 了 ！
He lay there for six **full** hours!

884 正   zhèng   **Adjective:** straight; upright

kuài bǎ yǐ zi fú zhèng
快 把 椅 子 扶 **正** 。
Straighten (hold **straight**) the chair quickly.

885 正式   zhèng shì   **Adjective:** formal

bú yào zài zhèng shì chǎng hé chuān tuō xié
不 要 在 **正 式** 场 合 穿 拖 鞋 。
Don't wear flip-flops on **formal** occasions.

886 证(件)   zhèng jiàn   **Noun:** certificate

wǒ men xū yào kàn de zhèng jiàn shì jià shǐ zhèng
我 们 需 要 看 的 **证 件** 是 驾 驶 证 。
The **certificate** we need to see is your driver's license.

887 证据 zhèng jù **Noun:** evidence

<ruby>监<rt>jiān</rt></ruby> <ruby>控<rt>kòng</rt></ruby> <ruby>器<rt>qì</rt></ruby> <ruby>的<rt>de</rt></ruby> <ruby>记<rt>jì</rt></ruby> <ruby>录<rt>lù</rt></ruby> <ruby>就<rt>jiù</rt></ruby> <ruby>是<rt>shì</rt></ruby> <ruby>他<rt>tā</rt></ruby> <ruby>的<rt>de</rt></ruby> <ruby>犯<rt>fàn</rt></ruby> <ruby>罪<rt>zuì</rt></ruby> <ruby>证<rt>zhèng</rt></ruby> <ruby>据<rt>jù</rt></ruby> 。
The CCTV record is his criminal **evidence**.

888 证明 zhèng míng **Verb:** to prove
Noun: proof

Verb
<ruby>你<rt>nǐ</rt></ruby> <ruby>怎<rt>zěn</rt></ruby> <ruby>么<rt>me</rt></ruby> <ruby>证<rt>zhèng</rt></ruby> <ruby>明<rt>míng</rt></ruby> <ruby>你<rt>nǐ</rt></ruby> <ruby>生<rt>shēng</rt></ruby> <ruby>在<rt>zài</rt></ruby> <ruby>美<rt>měi</rt></ruby> <ruby>国<rt>guó</rt></ruby> ？
How do you **prove** that you were born in the United States?

Noun
<ruby>这<rt>zhè</rt></ruby> <ruby>是<rt>shì</rt></ruby> <ruby>我<rt>wǒ</rt></ruby> <ruby>的<rt>de</rt></ruby> <ruby>出<rt>chū</rt></ruby> <ruby>生<rt>shēng</rt></ruby> <ruby>证<rt>zhèng</rt></ruby> <ruby>明<rt>míng</rt></ruby> 。
This is my birth **proof** (certificate).

889 支 zhī **Classifier** for thin and long objects

<ruby>我<rt>wǒ</rt></ruby> <ruby>买<rt>mǎi</rt></ruby> <ruby>了<rt>le</rt></ruby> <ruby>六<rt>liù</rt></ruby> <ruby>支<rt>zhī</rt></ruby> <ruby>彩<rt>cǎi</rt></ruby> <ruby>色<rt>sè</rt></ruby> <ruby>的<rt>de</rt></ruby> <ruby>铅<rt>qiān</rt></ruby> <ruby>笔<rt>bǐ</rt></ruby> 。
I bought six colored pencils.

890 支持 zhī chí **Verb:** to support
Noun: support

Verb
<ruby>我<rt>wǒ</rt></ruby> <ruby>们<rt>men</rt></ruby> <ruby>非<rt>fēi</rt></ruby> <ruby>常<rt>cháng</rt></ruby> <ruby>支<rt>zhī</rt></ruby> <ruby>持<rt>chí</rt></ruby> <ruby>儿<rt>ér</rt></ruby> <ruby>子<rt>zi</rt></ruby> <ruby>学<rt>xué</rt></ruby> <ruby>中<rt>zhōng</rt></ruby> <ruby>文<rt>wén</rt></ruby> 。
We **support** our son learning Chinese very much.

Noun
<ruby>谢<rt>xiè</rt></ruby> <ruby>谢<rt>xie</rt></ruby> <ruby>您<rt>nín</rt></ruby> <ruby>的<rt>de</rt></ruby> <ruby>支<rt>zhī</rt></ruby> <ruby>持<rt>chí</rt></ruby> ， <ruby>我<rt>wǒ</rt></ruby> <ruby>很<rt>hěn</rt></ruby> <ruby>感<rt>gǎn</rt></ruby> <ruby>激<rt>jī</rt></ruby> ！
Thank you for your **support**, I appreciate it!

891 支付 zhī fù **Verb:** to pay money; to defray

<ruby>请<rt>qǐng</rt></ruby> <ruby>大<rt>dà</rt></ruby> <ruby>家<rt>jiā</rt></ruby> <ruby>在<rt>zài</rt></ruby> <ruby>网<rt>wǎng</rt></ruby> <ruby>上<rt>shàng</rt></ruby> <ruby>支<rt>zhī</rt></ruby> <ruby>付<rt>fù</rt></ruby> <ruby>学<rt>xué</rt></ruby> <ruby>费<rt>fèi</rt></ruby> 。
May I ask everyone **to pay** tuition online.

892 直   zhí   **Adjective:** straight

_{wǒ} _{de} _{tóu} _{fā} _{bǐ} _{jiào} _{wān}   _{tā} _{de} _{bǐ} _{jiào} _{zhí}
我 的 头 发 比 较 弯 ， 她 的 比 较 **直** 。
My hair is relatively curly, hers is relatively **straight**.

893 直播   zhí bō   **Verb:** to live stream; to brodcast (live)

_{wǒ} _{zuì} _{xǐ} _{huān} _{de} _{bó} _{zhǔ} _{zài} _{zhí} _{bō}
我 最 喜 欢 的 博 主 在 **直 播** ！
My favorite blogger is **live streaming**.

894 直到   zhí dào   **Verb:** until

_{jīn} _{tiān} _{zǎo} _{shàng} _{wǒ} _{zhí} _{dào} _{shí} _{diǎn} _{cái} _{qǐ} _{chuáng}
今 天 早 上 我 **直 到** 十 点 才 起 床 。
I didn't get up **until** ten o'clock this morning.

895 值   zhí   **Verb:** to value; to be worth

_{zhè} _{kuài} _{biǎo} _{shì} _{míng} _{pái}   _{zhì} _{shǎo} _{zhí} _{yī} _{wàn} _{měi} _{yuán}
这 块 表 是 名 牌 ， 至 少 **值** 一 万 美 元 。
This watch is a famous brand, **worth** at least ten thousand dollars.

896 值得   zhí dé   **Verb:** to be worthy (not money related)

_{nà} _{zhǒng} _{bèn} _{dàn} _{bù} _{zhí} _{dé} _{nǐ} _{shēng} _{qì}
那 种 笨 蛋 不 **值 得** 你 生 气 。
That kind of idiot isn't **worth** your anger.

897 职工   zhí gōng   **Noun:** staff; worker

下 周 一 要 开 **职 工** 代 表 大 会 ， 你

xià zhōu yī yào kāi zhí gōng dài biǎo dà huì nǐ

参 加 吗 ？

cān jiā ma

There will be a **staff** representative conference next Monday, will you attend?

898 职业   zhí yè   **Noun:** occupation; vocation

我 建 议 我 妹 去 上 **职 业** 学 校 。

wǒ jiàn yì wǒ mèi qù shàng zhí yè xué xiào

I suggested to my younger sister to go attend a **vocational** school.

899 只好   zhǐ hǎo   **Adverb:** have to (no choice but to)

航 班 被 取 消 了 ， 我 **只 好** 坐 火 车 。

háng bān bèi qǔ xiāo le wǒ zhǐ hǎo zuò huǒ chē

The flight was canceled, so I **had to** take the train.

900 只是   zhǐ shì   **Adverb:** merely; just

我 **只 是** 不 太 习 惯 坐 十 个 小 时 的

wǒ zhǐ shì bú tài xí guàn zuò shí gè xiǎo shí de

火 车 。

huǒ chē

I'm **just** not used to a ten-hour train ride.

901 只(有)   zhǐ yǒu   **Adverb:** only

放 心 ， 我 永 远 **只** 爱 你 一 个 人 ！

fàng xīn wǒ yǒng yuǎn zhǐ ài nǐ yí gè rén

Rest assured, I will love **only** you forever!

902 (手)指   zhǐ   **Noun:** finger

jié hūn jiè zhǐ yīng gāi dài zài wú míng zhǐ shàng
结 婚 戒 指 应 该 戴 在 无 名 **指** 上 。
Wedding rings should be worn on the ring **finger**.

903 指出   zhǐ chū   **Verb:** to point out; to indicate

yǒu xiē rén tǎo yàn bèi zhí jiē zhǐ chū cuò wù
有 些 人 讨 厌 被 直 接 **指 出** 错 误 。
Some people dislike their mistakes being **pointed out** directly.

904 指导   zhǐ dǎo   **Verb:** to guide   **Noun:** guidance

Verb
má fán nǐ zhǐ dǎo wǒ men wán chéng fān yì
麻 烦 你 **指 导** 我 们 完 成 翻 译 。
Please **guide** us to complete the translation.

Noun
xiè xie nǐ de nài xīn hé zhǐ dǎo
谢 谢 你 的 耐 心 和 **指 导** 。
Thank you for your patience and **guidance**.

905 至今   zhì jīn   **Adverb:** so far

wǒ zhì jīn dōu bù xiāng xìn tā yǒu xiǎo sān
我 **至 今** 都 不 相 信 他 有 小 三 ！
I **so far** find hard to believe that he has a mistress!

906 至少   zhì shǎo   **Adverb:** at least

ér qiě tā zhì shǎo chū guǐ sì nián le
而 且 ， 他 **至 少** 出 轨 四 年 了 ！
Moreover, he has been cheating for **at least** four years!

907 志愿

zhì yuàn **Noun:** aspiration

dù jué bào lì shì wǒ men jī gòu de zhì yuàn
杜 绝 暴 力 是 我 们 机 构 的 **志 愿** 。
The elimination of violence is an **aspiration** of our institution.

908 志愿者

zhì yuàn zhě **Noun:** volunteer

wǒ men yí gòng yǒu wǔ shí míng zhì yuàn zhě
我 们 一 共 有 五 十 名 **志 愿 者** 。
We have fifty **volunteers** in total.

909 制定

zhì dìng **Verb:** to formulate

gōng sī de guǎn lǐ yuán zé shì zǒng cái zhì dìng de
公 司 的 管 理 原 则 是 总 裁 **制 定** 的 。
The company's governing principles are **formulated** by the CEO.

910 制度

zhì dù **Noun:** system

wǒ men jué de yīng gāi wán shàn guǎn lǐ zhì dù
我 们 觉 得 应 该 完 善 管 理 **制 度** 。
We feel that the management **system** should be refined.

911 制造

zhì zào

Verb: to make;
to manufacture
Noun: manufacture

Verb
zhè xiē jiā jù dōu shì zài zhōng guó zhì zào de
这 些 家 具 都 是 在 中 国 **制 造** 的 。
These furnitures are all **made** in China.

Noun
zhì zào háng yè zài xī fāng yuè lái yuè ruò
制 造 行 业 在 西 方 越 来 越 弱 。
The **manufacturing** sector is getting weaker in the West.

912 制作　　　　zhì zuò　　　**Verb:** to make (intangible thing)

制作 这 部 电 影 花 了 几 亿 美 元 。
zhì zuò zhè bù diàn yǐng huā le jǐ yì měi yuán

It took hundreds of millions of dollars **to make** the movie.

913 中部　　　　zhōng bù　　　**Noun:** central; middle part

他 的 家 乡 在 澳 大 利 亚 中 部 。
tā de jiā xiāng zài ào dà lì yà zhōng bù

His hometown is in **central** Australia.

914 中华民族　　zhōng huá mín zú　　**Noun:** Chinese ethnic

中 华 民 族 是 56 个 中 国 民 族 的 总 称 。
zhōng huá mín zú shì gè zhōng guó mín zú de zǒng chēng

The **Chinese ethnic** refers to the total 56 Chinese ethnic groups.

915 终于　　　　zhōng yú　　　**Adverb:** finally

我 的 考 试 终 于 过 了 ！
wǒ de kǎo shì zhōng yú guò le

I **finally** passed my exam!

916 钟　　　　zhōng　　　**Noun:** bell; clock

我 发 现 只 有 老 人 的 家 里 有 钟 。
wǒ fā xiàn zhǐ yǒu lǎo rén de jiā lǐ yǒu zhōng

I found that only old people's homes have **clocks**.

917a 种　　　　zhǒng　　　**Noun:** type; kind; species

我 不 喜 欢 吃 这 种 味 道 的 巧 克 力 。
wǒ bù xǐ huān chī zhè zhǒng wèi dào de qiǎo kè lì

I don't like to eat chocolate with this **kind** of taste.

917b 种   zhòng   **Verb:** to grow; to plant

wǒ xiǎng zài huā yuán zhòng yì kē yīng huā shù
我 想 在 花 园 **种** 一 颗 樱 花 树 。
I want **to plant** a cherry blossom tree in my garden.

918 种子   zhǒng zi   **Noun:** seed

zài nǎ lǐ kě yǐ mǎi yīng huā shù de zhǒng zi
在 哪 里 可 以 买 樱 花 树 的 **种 子** ？
Where can I buy cherry blossom tree **seeds**?

919 重大   zhòng dà   **Adjective:** significant

duì yǒu xiē rén ， bì yè diǎn lǐ de yì yì hěn
对 有 些 人 ， 毕 业 典 礼 的 意 义 很
zhòng dà
重 大 。
For some people, graduation ceremonies are very **significant**.

920 周围   zhōu wéi   **Noun:** around; surroundings

wǒ jiā zhōu wéi yǒu yì jiā zhōng cān wài mài diàn
我 家 **周 围** 有 一 家 中 餐 外 卖 店 。
There is a Chinese takeaway **around** (nearby) my house.

921 猪   zhū   **Noun:** pig

wǒ zài nà biān kàn dào le yì tóu yě zhū
我 在 那 边 看 到 了 一 头 野 **猪** 。
I saw a wild **pig** over there.

922 主持　　zhǔ chí　　**Verb:** to host

wǒ de guī mì huì bāng wǒ zhǔ chí shēng rì jù huì
我 的 闺 蜜 会 帮 我 **主 持** 生 日 聚 会 。
My best friend will **host** my birthday party for me.

923 主动　　zhǔ dòng　　**Adjective:** proactive; active (take initiative)

tā yǐ qián zuò shì hěn bèi dòng xiàn zài hěn zhǔ dòng
他 以 前 做 事 很 被 动 ， 现 在 很 **主 动** 。
He used to be very passive in doing things, but now he is very **proactive**.

924 主任　　zhǔ rèn　　**Noun:** headmaster; department head

wáng lǎo shī shì hàn yǔ xì de xīn zhǔ rèn
王 老 师 是 汉 语 系 的 新 **主 任** 。
Teacher Wang is the new **head** of the Chinese Language Department.

925 主意　　zhǔ yi　　**Noun:** idea

zài xué xiào qìng zhù chūn jié shì tā de zhǔ yi
在 学 校 庆 祝 春 节 是 他 的 **主 意** 。
It is his **idea** to celebrate the Spring Festival at school.

926 主张　　zhǔ zhāng　　**Verb:** to suggest; to propose　**Noun:** proposal

Verb
wǒ zhǔ zhāng wǒ men bān zǔ zhī gē wǔ biǎo yǎn
我 **主 张** 我 们 班 组 织 歌 舞 表 演 。
I **propose** that our class organize singing and dancing performances.

Noun
nǐ men zàn chéng zhè gè zhǔ zhāng ma
你 们 赞 成 这 个 **主 张** 吗 ？
Do you approve of this **proposal**?

927 注意   zhù yì   **Verb:** to be careful

wǒ zài dào chē，qǐng dà jiā zhù yì。
我 在 倒 车 ， 请 大 家 注 意 。

I'm reversing the car, please **be careful**.

928 祝   zhù   **Verb:** to wish

wǒ zhù nǐ shēng rì kuài lè！wàn shì rú yì！
我 祝 你 生 日 快 乐 ！ 万 事 如 意 ！

I **wish** you a happy birthday! May all go well with you!

929 抓(住)   zhuā zhù   **Verb:** to grab; grip; to arrest

tīng shuō， xiǎo tōu gāng gāng bèi jǐng chá zhuā zhù le。
听 说 ， 小 偷 刚 刚 被 警 察 抓 住 了 。

I heard that the thief was just **caught** by the police.

930 专家   zhuān jiā   **Noun:** expert

tā shì wǒ men yī yuàn zuì nián qīng de yī xué zhuān jiā。
他 是 我 们 医 院 最 年 轻 的 医 学 专 家 。

He is the youngest medical **expert** in our hospital.

931 专门   zhuān mén   **Adverb:** specifically (for a purpose)

wèi le ràng tā kāi xīn， wǒ zhuān mén gěi tā mǎi
为 了 让 她 开 心 ， 我 专 门 给 她 买
le yí shù méi guī。
了 一 束 玫 瑰 。

In order to make her happy, I **specifically** bought her a bouquet of roses.

932 专题   zhuān tí   **Noun:** specific topic (academic)

_{nǐ} _{zhī} _{dào} _{zhè} _{cì} _{biàn} _{lùn} _{de} _{zhuān} _{tí} _{shì} _{shén} _{me} _{ma}
你 知 道 这 次 辩 论 的 **专 题** 是 什 么 吗 ？
Do you know what the **specific topic** of this debate is?

933 专业   zhuān yè   **Noun:** major (academic)

_{zài} _{dà} _{xué} _{wǒ} _{de} _{zhuān} _{yè} _{shì} _{huà} _{xué}
在 大 学 ， 我 的 **专 业** 是 化 学 。
In university, my **major** was chemistry.

934a 转   zhuǎn   **Verb:** to turn

_{yì} _{zhí} _{zǒu} _{rán} _{hòu} _{zuǒ} _{zhuǎn} _{jiù} _{dào} _{le}
一 直 走 ， 然 后 左 **转** ， 就 到 了 。
Go straight, then **turn** left, and you're there.

934b 转   zhuàn   **Verb:** to revolve; to circulate

_{qí} _{shí} _{yuè} _{liàng} _{yì} _{zhí} _{wéi} _{zhe} _{dì} _{qiú} _{zhuàn}
其 实 ， 月 亮 一 直 围 着 地 球 **转** 。
In fact, the moon keeps **revolving** around the earth.

935 转变   zhuǎn biàn   **Verb:** to change (transform)
                                  Noun: transformation

Verb
_{zuì} _{jìn} _{jǐ} _{nián} _{tā} _{de} _{xìng} _{gé} _{zhuǎn} _{biàn} _{de} _{hěn} _{kuài}
最 近 几 年 ， 她 的 性 格 **转 变** 得 很 快 。
In recent years, her personality has **changed** rapidly.

Noun
_{hěn} _{duō} _{péng} _{yǒu} _{hěn} _{nán} _{jiē} _{shòu} _{tā} _{de} _{zhuǎn} _{biàn}
很 多 朋 友 很 难 接 受 她 的 **转 变** 。
Many friends had a hard time accepting her **transformation**.

936 状况　　zhuàng kuàng　**Noun: status; condition**

我 外 公 的 身 体 **状 况** 越 来 越 差 。
wǒ wài gōng de shēn tǐ zhuàngkuàng yuè lái yuè chā

My maternal grandfather's health **condition** is getting worse and worse.

937 状态　　zhuàng tài　**Noun: state (condition)**

但 是 他 很 乐 观 ， **状 态** 也 好 。
dàn shì tā hěn lè guān zhuàng tài yě hǎo

But he is optimistic and is also in a good **state**.

938 追　　zhuī　**Verb: to run after; to chase**

你 看 ， 我 的 狗 又 在 **追** 我 的 猫 。
nǐ kàn wǒ de gǒu yòu zài zhuī wǒ de māo

You see, my dog is **chasing** my cat again.

939 准　　zhǔn　**Verb: to permit; to allow**

我 不 **准** 我 的 儿 子 跟 女 儿 打 架 。
wǒ bù zhǔn wǒ de ér zi gēn nǚ ér dǎ jià

I don't **allow** my son to fight with my daughter.

940 资格　　zī gé　**Noun: eligibility; qualification**

委 员 会 恢 复 了 他 的 比 赛 **资 格** 。
wěi yuán huì huī fù le tā de bǐ sài zī gé

The committee reinstated his participating **eligibility**.

941 资金　　zī jīn　**Noun: capital or funds (money)**

有 些 贪 官 总 是 把 **资 金** 转 移 到 国 外 。
yǒu xiē tān guān zǒng shì bǎ zī jīn zhuǎn yí dào guó wài

Some corrupt officials always transfer **captital** abroad.

942 子女   zǐ nǚ   **Noun:** sons and daughters

tā qù shì hòu, zǐ nǚ jì chéng le tā de quán bù
他 去 世 后 ， **子 女** 继 承 了 他 的 全 部
zī chǎn
资 产 。

After he passed away, his **sons and daughters** inherited all his assets.

943 自从   zì cóng   **Preposition:** since

zì cóng fēn shǒu hòu, tā men jiù méi yǒu lián xì
自 从 分 手 后 ， 他 们 就 没 有 联 系
guò duì fāng
过 对 方 。

Since breaking up, they haven't been in touch with each other.

944 自动   zì dòng   **Adjective:** automatic

wǒ zài shǒu jī shàng shè zhì le zì dòng kāi jī hé
我 在 手 机 上 设 置 了 **自 动** 开 机 和
guān jī
关 机 。

I set **automatic** power on and off on my phone.

945 自觉   zì jué   **Adjective:** self-conscious (to avoid bad consequences)

wǒ nǚ ér zuì jìn zǎo shuì zǎo qǐ, fēi cháng zì jué
我 女 儿 最 近 早 睡 早 起 ， 非 常 **自 觉** 。

My daughter goes to bed early and gets up early recently, very **self-conscious**.

946 自然　zì rán　**Adjective:** natural
Noun: nature

Adj.

nǐ nà me měi　tā bèi nǐ xī yǐn hěn zì rán
你 那 么 美 ！ 他 被 你 吸 引 很 **自 然** 。
You are so beautiful! It's **natural** for him to be attracted to you.

Noun

bǎo hù zì rán shì měi gè rén de zé rèn
保 护 **自 然** 是 每 个 人 的 责 任 。
Protecting **nature** is everyone's responsibility.

947 自身　zì shēn　**Noun:** oneself;
one's own

tā bú gù zì shēn ān quán　tiào xià shuǐ qù jiù
他 不 顾 **自 身** 安 全 ， 跳 下 水 去 救
hái zi
孩 子 。
He ignored his **own** safety and jumped into the water to save the
child.

948 自主　zì zhǔ　**Verb:**
to act on one's own

yǒu xiē shāng diàn kě yǐ lì yòng rén gōng zhì néng zì
有 些 商 店 可 以 利 用 人 工 智 能 **自**
zhǔ jīng yíng
主 经 营 。
Some stores can operate **on their own** using artificial intelligence.

949 总结　zǒng jié　**Verb:** to summarize
Noun: summary

Verb

qǐng zǒng jié chuàng yè de hǎo chù hé huài chù
请 **总 结** 创 业 的 好 处 和 坏 处 。
Please **summarize** the pros and cons of starting a business.

Noun

dà jiā duì tā de zǒng jié bào gào hěn mǎn yì
大 家 对 他 的 **总 结** 报 告 很 满 意 。
Everyone is very satisfied with his **summary** report.

950 总(是)   zǒng shì   **Adverb:** always

tā èr shí duō suì de shí hòu   zǒng shì qù yè diàn
他 二 十 多 岁 的 时 候 ，**总 是 去 夜 店** 。
When he was in his twenties, he **always** went to nightclubs.

951 (足)够   zú gòu   **Verb:** enough; sufficient

tā fā míng le zhè gè ruǎn jiàn   què shí zú gòu
他 发 明 了 这 个 软 件 ， 确 实 **足 够**
cōng míng
聪 明 ！
He invented this software, truly smart **enough**!

952 足球   zú qiú   **Noun:** soccer; football

wǒ de péng yǒu men dōu shì zú qiú mí
我 的 朋 友 们 都 是 **足 球** 迷 。
My friends are all **football** fans.

953 组合   zǔ hé   **Noun:** group; combination

zhè tiáo qún zi de yán sè shì lán sè hé lǜ sè
这 条 裙 子 的 颜 色 是 蓝 色 和 绿 色
de zǔ hé
的 **组 合** 。
The color of this skirt is a **combination** of blue and green.

954 左右   zuǒ yòu   **Adverb:** about; approximately

tā de jià gé yǒu diǎn guì   zài liǎng bǎi měi yuán
它 的 价 格 有 点 贵 ， 在 两 百 美 元
zuǒ yòu
左 右 。
It's price is a bit expensive, **about** two hundred dollars.

955 作品   zuò pǐn   **Noun:** work (literature and art)

wǒ fēi cháng xīn shǎng tā de yì shù zuò pǐn
我 非 常 欣 赏 她 的 艺 术 **作 品** 。
I really admire her art**work**.

956 作者   zuò zhě   **Noun:** author

zhè běn xiǎo shuō de zuò zhě shì èr shí shì jì de
这 本 小 说 的 **作 者** 是 二 十 世 纪 的
míng rén
名 人 。
The **author** of this novel is a celebrity of the twentieth century.

957 做客   zuò kè   **Verb:** to be a guest

wǒ men míng tiān huì qù běi jīng de péng yǒu jiā zuò kè
我 们 明 天 会 去 北 京 的 朋 友 家 **做 客** 。
We will **be guests** of our friend's house in Beijing tomorrow.

2

KEY GRAMMAR
IN CONTEXT

subject + 就^{jiù} (是^{shì}) + verb

used to add emphasis
(just/simply/right away)

Ex. 1

我^{wǒ} 就^{jiù} 是^{shì} 想^{xiǎng} 知^{zhī} 道^{dào} 她^{tā} 到^{dào} 底^{dǐ} 爱^{ài} 不^{bú} 爱^{ài} 我^{wǒ} 。

I **just** want to know if she loves me or not after all.

Ex. 2

别^{bié} 担^{dān} 心^{xīn} ， 我^{wǒ} 们^{men} 十^{shí} 分^{fēn} 钟^{zhōng} 后^{hòu} 就^{jiù} 到^{dào} 。

Don't worry, we'll arrive **right away** in ten minutes.

就^{jiù} + verb phrase

then/in that case

Ex. 3

如^{rú} 果^{guǒ} 你^{nǐ} 愿^{yuàn} 意^{yì} ， 我^{wǒ} 们^{men} 就^{jiù} 明^{míng} 年^{nián} 结^{jié} 婚^{hūn} 。

If you are willing, **then** let's get married next year.

就^{jiù} + (subject) + predicate

only/just

Ex. 4

这^{zhè} 次^{cì} 聚^{jù} 餐^{cān} ，就^{jiù} 我^{wǒ} 们^{men} 四^{sì} 个^{gè} 人^{rén} 参^{cān} 加^{jiā} 。

This time's dinner party, **only** four of us attended.

Write your own:

② 对... 有/感 兴趣

A + 对 + B + 有 / 感 兴 趣
duì   yǒu gǎn xìng qù

to express interest in something
(interested in...)

Ex. 1
这 个 花 花 公 子 只 对 美 女 有 兴 趣 。
zhè gè huā huā gōng zǐ zhǐ duì měi nǚ yǒu xìng qù

This playboy is only **interested in** beautiful women.

Ex. 2
其 实 ， 她 对 打 篮 球 不 感 兴 趣 。
qí shí   tā duì dǎ lán qiú bù gǎn xìng qù

In fact, she is not **interested in** playing basketball.

Write your own:

③ （以）后...

time/event + （ 以 ） 后 + clause
yǐ hòu

to express sequence of events
(after...)

Ex. 1
吃 完 饭 后 ， 我 们 去 河 边 散 步 吧 。
chī wán fàn hòu   wǒ men qù hé biān sàn bù ba

After we finish dinner, let's go for a walk by the river.

Ex. 2
毕 业 以 后 ， 我 们 很 少 联 系 对 方 。
bì yè yǐ hòu   wǒ men hěn shǎo lián xì duì fāng

After graduation, we rarely contacted each other.

Write your own:

④ 不是... 就是...

不 是 +A+ 就 是 +B　　　　**either... or...**

bú shì　jiù shì

Ex. 1
他 不 是 在 骗 你，就 是 在 开 玩 笑 。

tā bú shì zài piàn nǐ　jiù shì zài kāi wán xiào

He's **either** lying to you, **or** joking.

Ex. 2
这 次 的 冠 军 不 是 法 国 队 就 是

zhè cì de guàn jūn bú shì fǎ guó duì jiù shì

德 国 队 。

dé guó duì

This time's champion will be **either** the French team **or** German team.

Write your own:

⑤ 不仅... 还...

不 仅 +A+ 还 +B　　　　**not only... but also...**

bù jǐn　hái

Ex. 1
我 不 仅 喜 欢 旅 游，还 喜 欢 交 朋 友 。

wǒ bù jǐn xǐ huān lǚ yóu hái xǐ huān jiāo péng yǒu

I **not only** like to travel, **but also** like to make friends.

Ex. 2
他 不 仅 是 我 的 爱 人 ， 还 是 我 最

tā bù jǐn shì wǒ de ài rén　hái shì wǒ zuì

好 的 朋 友 。

hǎo de péng yǒu

He is **not only** my spouse, **but** also my best friend.

Write your own:

⑥ 可是... 却...

clause + 可 是 + subject + 却 + verb
_{kě} _{shì} _{què}

used to express contrast between
two ideas or situations
(but/yet...)

Ex. 1
虽 然 结 婚 了 ， **可 是** 他 **却** 有 情 人 。
suī rán jié hūn le kě shì tā què yǒu qíng rén

Although married, **yet** he has a mistress.

Ex. 2
明 天 就 会 签 合 同 ， **可 是** 他 **却** 很
míng tiān jiù huì qiān hé tóng kě shì tā què hěn
犹 豫 。
yóu yù

The contract will be signed tomorrow, **but** he is hesitating.

Write your own:

⑦ ...极了

adjective + 极 了
_{jí} _{le}

used to express a high degree of a
particular quality or characteristic
(extremely...)

Ex. 1
她 是 个 天 才 ， 艺 术 作 品 都 美 **极 了** ！
tā shì gè tiān cái yì shù zuò pǐn dōu měi jí le

She is a genius and her artworks are all **extremely** beautiful.

Ex. 2
狗 看 到 我 回 家 的 时 候 ， 激 动 **极 了** 。
gǒu kàn dào wǒ huí jiā de shí hòu jī dòng jí le

When the dog saw me coming home, he was **extremely** excited.

Write your own:

⑧ 就要...了

subject + 就要 (jiù yào) + verb + 了 (le)

an event/action is about to happen
(about to...)

Ex. 1
我 (wǒ) 就 (jiù) 要 (yào) 下 (xià) 班 (bān) 了 (le) ，你 (nǐ) 明 (míng) 天 (tiān) 再 (zài) 来 (lái) 报 (bào) 名 (míng) 吧 (ba) 。

I'm **about to** get off work, please come to sign up again tomorrow.

Ex. 2
听 (tīng) 说 (shuō) 这 (zhè) 部 (bù) 电 (diàn) 视 (shì) 剧 (jù) 下 (xià) 个 (gè) 月 (yuè) 就 (jiù) 要 (yào) 播 (bō) 出 (chū) 了 (le) 。

I heard that the TV series is **about to** air next month.

Write your own:

⑨ 和...交朋友

A + 和 (hé) + B + 交朋友 (jiāo péng yǒu)

to make friends with

Ex. 1
他 (tā) 曾 (céng) 经 (jīng) 很 (hěn) 喜 (xǐ) 欢 (huān) **和** (hé) **陌** (mò) **生** (shēng) **人** (rén) **交** (jiāo) **朋** (péng) **友** (yǒu) 。

He used to like **making friends with** strangers.

Ex. 2
你 (nǐ) 知 (zhī) 道 (dào) 怎 (zěn) 样 (yàng) **和** (hé) **成** (chéng) **功** (gōng) **的** (de) **人** (rén) **交** (jiāo) **朋** (péng) **友** (yǒu) 吗 (ma) ？

Do you know how **to make friends with** successful people?

Write your own:

⑩ 和...绝交

A + 和 hé + B + 绝交 jué jiāo

to break ties with...

Ex. 1

我 wǒ 不 bù 喜 xǐ 欢 huān 在 zài 公 gōng 共 gòng 场 chǎng 合 hé 和 hé 朋 péng 友 yǒu 绝 jué 交 jiāo 。

I don't like **to break ties with** friends in public places.

Ex. 2

自 zì 从 cóng 上 shàng 次 cì 和 hé 他 tā 吵 chǎo 架 jià 后 hòu ， 我 wǒ 就 jiù 和 hé 他 tā 绝 jué 交 jiāo 了 le 。

Since the last fight with him, I have **broken ties with** him.

Write your own:

⑪ ...得...

verb + 得 de + adjective

used to describe how an action is performed to a certain degree

Ex. 1

和 hé 男 nán 朋 péng 友 yǒu 分 fēn 手 shǒu 后 hòu ， 她 tā 哭 kū 得 de 很 hěn 伤 shāng 心 xīn 。

After breaking up with her boyfriend, she cried very sadly.

Ex. 2

他 tā 处 chǔ 理 lǐ 客 kè 户 hù 问 wèn 题 tí 处 chǔ 理 lǐ 得 de 非 fēi 常 cháng 好 hǎo ！

He handles customer issues very well!

Write your own:

194

⑫ ...一下

verb + 一下
_{yí xià}

indicates a brief, quick, or casual attempt or action
(**a bit/quickly...**)

Ex. 1

我 觉 得 很 累， 想 休 息 一 下 。
_{wǒ jué de hěn lèi, xiǎng xiū xī yí xià}

I feel very tired and want to rest **a bit**.

Ex. 2

我 介 绍 一 下， 这 是 我 们 代 表 团
_{wǒ jiè shào yí xià, zhè shì wǒ men dài biǎo tuán}
的 主 席 王 先 生 。
_{de zhǔ xí wáng xiān shēng}

Let me introduce **quickly**, this is the chairman of our delegation, Mr. Wang.

Write your own:

⑬ 当...(是)...

A + 当 + B + (是) + noun
_{dāng}   _{shì}

to treat/regard ... as ...

Ex. 1

其 实， 我 一 直 把 房 东 当 我 的 好
_{qí shí, wǒ yì zhí bǎ fáng dōng dāng wǒ de hǎo}
朋 友 。
_{péng yǒu}

In fact, I have always **regarded** my landlord **as** my good friend.

Ex. 2

导 演 说 在 表 演 的 时 候， 要 当 自
_{dǎo yǎn shuō zài biǎo yǎn de shí hòu, yào dāng zì}
己 是 故 事 中 的 人 。
_{jǐ shì gù shi zhōng de rén}

The director said that when acting, you should **treat** yourself **as** the person in the story.

Write your own:

subject + 看_{kàn}上_{shàng}去_{qù}像_{xiàng} + noun

... looks like ...

Ex. 1
这_{zhè}个_{gè}歌_{gē}手_{shǒu}看_{kàn}上_{shàng}去_{qù}像_{xiàng}我_{wǒ}的_{de}一_{yí}个_{gè}
大_{dà}学_{xué}同_{tóng}学_{xué}。

This singer **looks like** one of my college classmates.

Ex. 2
这_{zhè}条_{tiáo}高_{gāo}速_{sù}公_{gōng}路_{lù}看_{kàn}上_{shàng}去_{qù}像_{xiàng}一_{yì}条_{tiáo}龙_{lóng}！

This expressway **looks like** a dragon!

Write your own:

要_{yào}是_{shì} + condition + 就_{jiù} + result

used to form a conditional
statement
(if... then...)

Ex. 1
要_{yào}是_{shì}我_{wǒ}有_{yǒu}钱_{qián}，我_{wǒ}就_{jiù}会_{huì}买_{mǎi}头_{tóu}等_{děng}舱_{cāng}
的_{de}机_{jī}票_{piào}。

If I had money, (**then**) I'd buy a first-class plane ticket.

Ex. 2
要_{yào}是_{shì}客_{kè}户_{hù}不_{bù}满_{mǎn}意_{yì}，就_{jiù}会_{huì}停_{tíng}止_{zhǐ}和_{hé}
我_{wǒ}们_{men}的_{de}合_{hé}作_{zuò}。

If the client is not satisfied, (**then**) they will stop the cooperation with us.

Write your own:

⑯ 对...有影响

A + 对^{duì} + B + 有^{yǒu} + (adj) + 影 响^{yǐng xiǎng}

to express one thing having an influence or impact on another
(has effect/impact on...)

Ex. 1

工 作 上 的 竞 争 对 我 们 的 关 系
^{gōng zuò shàng de jìng zhēng duì wǒ men de guān xi}
有 影 响 。
^{yǒu yǐng xiǎng}

Competition at work **has an effect on** our relationship.

Ex. 2

美 国 的 大 选 对 世 界 有 大 的 影 响 。
^{měi guó de dà xuǎn duì shì jiè yǒu dà de yǐng xiǎng}

The U.S. presidential election **has** a big **impact on** the world.

Write your own:

⑰ 对...来说

对^{duì} + someone + 来 说^{lái shuō} + clause

used to introduce opinions based on a specific entity's perspective
(for/from one's perspective...)

Ex. 1

对 我 来 说 ， 健 康 和 快 乐 是 最
^{duì wǒ lái shuō， jiàn kāng hé kuài lè shì zuì}
重 要 的 。
^{zhòng yào de}

For me, health and happiness are the most important.

Ex. 2

对 她 来 说 ， 她 的 狗 是 她 最 忠
^{duì tā lái shuō， tā de gǒu shì tā zuì zhōng}
诚 的 朋 友 。
^{chéng de péng yǒu}

From her **perspective**, her dog is her most loyal friend.

Write your own:

⑱ 除了...还(有)...

除了 chú le +A+ 还(有) hái yǒu +B   **besides/except...also**

Ex. 1

下班后，我除了要做饭，还要照顾孩子。
xià bān hòu, wǒ chú le yào zuò fàn, hái yào zhào gù hái zi

After I get off work, **besides** cooking, I **also** need to take care of the children.

Ex. 2

参加会议的除了人事部门，还有财经部门。
cān jiā huì yì de chú le rén shì bù mén, hái yǒu cái jīng bù mén

Besides the personnel department, the financial department **also** participated in the meeting.

Write your own:

⑲ 为了...

为了 wèi le + purpose + clause   used to provide insight into the reason behind an action **(in order to/for...)**

Ex. 1

为了提高口语，我每天早上大声朗读文章。
wéi le tí gāo kǒu yǔ, wǒ měi tiān zǎo shàng dà shēng lǎng dú wén zhāng

In order to improve my speaking, I read the article aloud every morning.

Ex. 2

为了集中注意力，我把手机静音了。
wéi le jí zhōng zhù yì lì, wǒ bǎ shǒu jī jìng yīn le

In order to concentrate my attention, I muted my phone.

Write your own:

⑳ 不是...而是...

不 是 _{bú shì} + A + 而 是 _{ér shì} + B

not... but...

Ex. 1

^{qí} ^{shí} ^{tā} ^{zuì} ^{ài} ^{de} ^{bú} ^{shì} ^{wǒ} ^{ér} ^{shì}
其 实 ， 他 最 爱 的 不 是 我 ， 而 是
^{tā} ^{zì} ^{jǐ}
他 自 己 。

In fact, who he loves most is **not** me, **but** himself.

Ex. 2

^{zhè} ^{gè} ^{jiàn} ^{yì} ^{bú} ^{shì} ^{wǒ} ^{tí} ^{de} ^{ér} ^{shì} ^{zhāng}
这 个 建 议 不 是 我 提 的 ， 而 是 张
^{hóng} ^{tí} ^{de}
红 提 的 。

This suggestion was **not** proposed by me, **but** by Zhang Hong.

Write your own:

ACCESS AUDIO

Please follow the instructions provided below to access the Chinese audio for this book:

INSTRUCTIONS TO ACCESS AUDIO

1. **Scan this QR code**
    or go to: www.linglingmandarin.com/books

2. Locate this book in the list of LingLing Mandarin Books

3. Click the "Access Audio" button

    Access Audio

4. Enter the password:

    ## NPAZ8

NEW HSK VOCABULARY SERIES

LEARN CHINESE
VOCABULARY FOR
BEGINNERS:
NEW HSK 1

LEARN CHINESE
VOCABULARY FOR
BEGINNERS:
NEW HSK 2

LEARN CHINESE
VOCABULARY FOR
BEGINNERS:
NEW HSK 3

LEARN CHINESE
VOCABULARY FOR
INTERMEDIATE:
NEW HSK 4

LEARN CHINESE
VOCABULARY FOR
INTERMEDIATE:
NEW HSK 5

LEARN CHINESE
VOCABULARY FOR
INTERMEDIATE:
NEW HSK 6

Get notified about **new releases**
https://linglingmandarin.com/notify

BOOKS BY LINGLING

**CHINESE
CONVERSATIONS**
FOR BEGINNERS

**CHINESE
CONVERSATIONS**
FOR INTERMEDIATE

MANDARIN WRITING
PRACTICE BOOK

CHINESE STORIES
FOR LANGUAGE
LEARNERS:
ELEMENTARY

CHINESE STORIES
FOR LANGUAGE
LEARNERS:
INTERMEDIATE

THE ART OF WAR
FOR LANGUAGE
LEARNERS

Get notified about **new releases**
https://linglingmandarin.com/notify

ABOUT THE AUTHOR

LingLing is a native Chinese Mandarin educator with an MA in Communication and Language. Originally from China, now living in the UK, she is the founder of the learning brand LingLing Mandarin, which aims to create the best resources for learners to master the Chinese language and achieve deep insight into Chinese culture in a fun and illuminating way. *Discover more about LingLing and access more great resources by following the links below or scanning the QR codes.*

 WEBSITE
linglingmandarin.com

YOUTUBE
youtube.com/c/linglingmandarin

 PATREON
patreon.com/linglingmandarin

INSTAGRAM
instagram.com/linglingmandarin